Botanica's
100 Best
FLOWERING
SHRUBS
FOR YOUR GARDEN

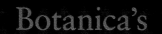

Botanica's
100 Best

FLOWERING
SHRUBS

FOR YOUR GARDEN

LAUREL
GLEN

First published in 2001 in North America by
Laurel Glen Publishing
An imprint of the Advantage Publishers Group
5880 Oberlin Drive, San Diego, CA 92121–4794
www.advantagebooksonline.com

Text © Random House Australia Pty Ltd 2001
Photos © Random House Australia Pty Ltd 2001
from the Random House Photo Library

All notions of errors or omissions should be addresed to
Laurel Glen Publishing, editorial department, at the above
address. Other correspondence (author inquiries, permissions
and rights) concerning the content of this book should be
addressed to Random House Australia, 20 Alfred Street,
Milsons Point, NSW 2061

ISBN 1-57145-482-9
Library of Congress Cataloging-in-Publication Data
available on request.

1 2 3 4 5   01 02 03 04 05

Publisher: **James Mills-Hicks**
Managing editor: **Susan Page**
Editor: **Jane Warren**
Publishing assistant: **Anabel Pandiella**
Consultant: **Geoff Bryant**
Page makeup: **Southern Star Design**
Production manager: **Linda Watchorn**
Film separation: **Pica Colour Separation, Singapore**
Printed by: **Dah Hua Printing Co. Ltd, Hong Kong**

Contents

INTRODUCTION

Shrubs—that vast and hugely diverse group of plants—create the stable framework of the garden and provide a strong visual backdrop to the transient elements of the garden. The group includes some of the most hardy and undemanding plants available, and their relative longevity means that they will delight for season after season. Their height, shape and form varies from those with a low-growing, trailing habit to those with an upright or even climbing habit, while those which also produce flowers, or a pleasant scent, are particularly rewarding.

Shrubs may be either evergreen or deciduous, although a shrub that is deciduous in its cold-climate natural habitat may be semideciduous in a more temperate climate. This means that it may never be entirely dormant, and it may put on a less brilliant autumn display, although the vitality of the plant will not be adversely affected.

Evergreens provide a reliable source of color, without which the winter garden would be barren indeed. But the late winter, spring or summer flowers, berries and autumn leaf displays of deciduous shrubs bring special joy to a garden, and it is therefore important to include both evergreen and deciduous shrubs when planning a garden. Deciduous shrubs look their best when planted in combination with—and preferably in front of—evergreens, while variegated forms of evergreens relieve the monotony of all-green foliage. With careful planning, therefore, it is possible to achieve year-round color and interest in the garden using a combination of flowering shrubs, both deciduous and evergreen. Remember that even

Specimen camellias in all their spring splendor.

evergreens will lose some leaves during periods of new growth—or simply on windy days—so, evergreen or not, be prepared to rake leaves!

When it comes to compiling a short list and selecting plants, choose those suited to your climate and soil type, and it is a good idea to take note, as you walk or drive about, of the flowering shrubs that thrive in your area. Find out the pH of your soil and establish whether it has a sandy or clay consistency. Be practical: there is no point in trying to persuade *Hibiscus* to grow outdoors in a cool, temperate climate; similarly, lilac *(Syringa)* prefers cold winters, with at least a few frosts, and will not thrive in relentlessly hot, dry conditions. Some shrubs are more exacting than others, and will flourish only if their particular soil and climate needs are met; others will adapt to less than ideal conditions.

Before you plant any shrub, it is essential to consider the height and width of the mature specimen and its rate of growth, as well as its characteristic shape, leaf color and flowering times.

A word of warning: don't be tempted to overplant your garden. Allow the shrubs enough space to spread and reach their full size without crowding each other. It

This well-planned border is a mass of color.

may take longer for your garden to become established, but your patience will be amply rewarded in time by the size and vigor of the plants.

Use in the garden

The position of your chosen shrubs is all-important. Grown not only for their height, shape, flowers, fragrance or foliage, shrubs can also act as a living screen. Large shrubs grown along fences and boundaries, either as a hedge or as a specimen plant, can provide privacy from neighbors or passersby. It is never advisable, however, to create a solid border of shrubs around a property. Not only does this look rigid and very formal, but boxing in the garden in this way makes it appear smaller and, particularly in narrow gardens, gradually reduces the available light as the tall shrubs grow even taller. There are desirable views from every garden and, by leaving judicious gaps in your border plantings, you will be able to enjoy the beautiful plants in nearby properties, without compromising your neighbors or your own privacy.

Landscape gardeners know that grouping plants—in odd numbers of 3 or more—enhances the flowers or foliage of a favorite plant, and gives substance and unity to a planting. Large garden beds, which can otherwise look patchy, benefit in particular from this treatment.

Remember that while a deciduous shrub planted outside a bedroom may provide a pleasant screen in summer (yet allowing light to penetrate in the winter), a dense evergreen bush in the same position will block out light and views from the room, all year round. Consider, too, where the

shadow of a large shrub will fall: a shady lawn may afford some relief during a hot summer, but deep shade could ruin a potentially sunny conservatory in winter. Fortunately, shrubs are easily transplanted, so any mistakes can be rectified!

Fragrant shrubs often have modest flowers, but since the scent of many, such as *Daphne*, will carry, they need not necessarily be planted in a prime spot near a patio or path. Others, like the lavender, are best planted where passersby can inadvertently brush against the foliage, thereby releasing the fragrance.

Growing habits and effects

Flowering shrubs are grown for a range of different effects. The specimen shrub, allowed to grow unhindered to full maturity, is probably the most common. However, superb results can be achieved when shrubs are pruned to shape, whether simply for effect, or in order to confine their growth in a small garden. Tender shrubs can be successfully espaliered against a wall where they will enjoy the shelter and still bear flowers or fruit. A courtyard makes an ideal setting for an espaliered flowering shrub.

Container planting is another option for flowering shrubs.

Erica carnea 'Myretoun Ruby'

Springtime—and these formal gardens are ablaze with colorful *Rhododendron*.

Azaleas, camellias, and some roses make superb container plants, providing they are not allowed to dry out. Standard flowering shrubs, which are popular in more formal gardens, have had their side shoots removed, the straight stem rising to a crown of foliage at the top. Standard roses may be traditional, but it is worth the effort of painstaking pruning and training—and the wait—to create your own favorites. Fuchsias are particularly versatile plants: they may be grown in the garden, in containers or hanging baskets, and they make especially colorful standards.

Hedges are commonly used to screen off the garden, or a part of it. A good hedge also makes an effective windbreak and will cut down the noise, dust and pollution from a busy street. While "hedge" was synonymous, in days gone by, with cypress and privet,

hedges today reflect the trend away from formal plantings. Instead of a uniform "wall" of evergreen foliage, the hedge can be designed as a visual treat using flowering species such as rhododendrons, flowering quince *(Chaenomeles)*, mock orange *(Philadelphus)* and roses in combination with attractive foliage plants.

Starting out... and getting results

Flowering shrubs can be bought at varying stages of maturity from garden centers and nurseries. Although it is tempting to buy large plants, which have immediate visual impact, it is usually advisable to use younger plants, whose rapid root growth will help them to become established more quickly.

Planting a shrub involves, firstly, the careful selection of a site: the soil should be well drained and there should be no standing water, although the soil in both the garden and container should be moist. Dig a hole deep enough for the root mass to be as deep as it was in the container. The hole should be about twice the width of the root mass, to allow plenty of room for the roots to spread out. Make a slight mound in the base of the hole, to direct the roots downwards. Position a stake, if necessary, at this stage. Place the root ball in the hole with the stem alongside the stake and be careful not to disturb the roots unduly. Replace the soil and press down firmly. With open or bare-rooted plants, gently tease the roots out over the base mound and replace the soil, pressing down to dispel any air bubbles but avoiding damage to the roots. Finally, replace the rest of the soil and with the excess, form a ridge about 12 in (30 cm) from the stem—this will stop water running off too quickly.

Staking protects young shrubs from wind damage while they are becoming established, and helps them grow straight. Place the stake—on the windward side of the shrub—at the time of planting, to avoid damage to the roots, or replace a stake by driving a new one in behind the old one.

A certain amount of movement is necessary for normal root growth, so don't lash the tree too tightly to the stake. Use wide ties, preferably of canvas or rubber, which will not cut into or chafe the stem as it moves and grows.

Keep the soil moist during the growing season. A good soaking, though time-consuming, is preferable to frequent light sprinklings of water, if the tap roots, and not merely the surface roots, are to be reached.

Mulching the base of the shrub protects the roots from extremes of temperature and drought. The natural mulches, such as bark chips, coir or grass clippings, are the best.

The best time for pruning will depend on the plant in question. Always use sharp tools; make a clean diagonal cut just above and opposite the growth bud; and, to direct new growth, cut above a bud that faces in the desired direction.

Pests and diseases vary depending on the plant and the climate, so approach your local garden center or nursery for advice if the condition of a plant deteriorates. In general, a plant enjoying ideal growing conditions will be less susceptible to disease than one that is forced to adapt to growing conditions that are not ideal.

AB

ABELIA

A genus of about 30 species of deciduous and evergreen shrubs from eastern Asia and Mexico, abelias are elegant and bear abundant small, tubular or trumpet-shaped flowers throughout the summer. They grow to about 6 ft (1.8 m) tall and have dark green foliage on arching canes. **CULTIVATION** Species vary from moderately frost hardy to somewhat tender. Frost-hardy species are trouble-free plants, capable of surviving harsh conditions. Abelias prefer sun or light shade, and need a well-drained soil with regular water in summer. Easily propagated from cuttings, they can withstand heavy pruning, for example, for low hedging.

Abelia × grandiflora

This hybrid between *Abelia chinensis* and *A. uniflora* grows 6–8 ft (1.8–2.4 m) tall and wide. It has arching, reddish brown canes and small, glossy, dark green leaves. Small mauve and white flowers appear in early summer, usually with a second flush at summer's end. The dull pink calyces persist after the flowers fall, contrasting with the leaves that turn purplish bronze. The cultivar 'Francis Mason' has yellow or yellow-edged leaves, although it has a tendency to revert to plain green. ZONES 7–10.

Abelia schumannii

Less vigorous than *Abelia × grandiflora*, this deciduous shrub likes a sheltered situation. It has arching red canes and small, pointed leaves; the upper part of each cane produces a succession of showy, bell-shaped

Abelia × grandiflora

Abelia schumannii cultivar

flowers from late spring to early autumn. The rose-pink flowers have an orange blotch in the throat; pale reddish calyces persist on the shrub after the flowers fall. ZONES 7–10.

ABELIOPHYLLUM

White forsythia

This genus, related to *Forsythia*, contains only one species—a deciduous shrub from Korea. It bears fragrant flowers from late winter into spring.
CULTIVATION White forsythias like fertile, well-drained soil and a position in full sun. Watch out for late frosts that can damage the blooms. Propagate from semi-ripe cuttings in summer.

Abeliophyllum distichum

This slow-growing, spreading shrub bears attractive, scented white flowers that are sometimes tinged

pink. In cooler areas, grow against a sunny wall; it reaches a height of about 5 ft (1.5 m). ZONES 5–9.

ABUTILON

syn. *Corynabutilon*
Chinese lantern, flowering maple

There are 100 or more species of mostly evergreen shrubs in this genus, but only a few truly merit the name "Chinese lantern;" that is, only a few have flowers pendent on weak stalks and an inflated calyx above a bell of 5 overlapping petals. A flower type such as this is adapted to pollination by hummingbirds. Most species, however, have a wide open flower like a small *Hibiscus*, with petals most commonly yellow or orange. Distributed widely through warmer countries, South America is home to most species. A small group of species from the cooler parts of Chile has mauve flowers and deciduous foliage, and is sometimes placed in a separate genus, *Corynabutilon*.
CULTIVATION They need well-drained soil and part-shade or full sun. In cooler climates, they can be grown in greenhouses or in containers in sheltered, sunny spots. They need good watering, especially if in containers (in which they bloom best if root-bound).

Propagate from cuttings in late summer. Flea-beetles, aphids and caterpillars can be a problem.

Abutilon × hybridum
Chinese lantern

Abutilon × hybridum is a collective name for cultivars derived from the hybridizing of some South American species. The lantern-like flowers, borne from spring to autumn, come in yellow, white, orange, pink, mauve and scarlet. Named cultivars include 'Nabob'; 'Ruby Glow'; 'Golden Fleece', 'Orange King'; 'Kentish Belle', with yellowish petals and a purple-red calyx; 'Ashford Red', a free flowering hybrid with luminous flowers; and 'Souvenir de Bonn', with variegated foliage and red-veined orange flowers. In warm climates they grow to 8 ft (2.4 m), some with a similar spread, and an open growth habit. Prune hard in early spring; tip prune to promote

Abutilon × hybridum

bushiness and flowering. These cultivars can be grown indoors in a cool but sunny room. ZONES 9–11.

Abutilon vitifolium
syn. *Corynabutilon vitifolium*

This soft-wooded, short-lived, deciduous shrub from Chile grows to 10–12 ft (3–3.5 m). In summer it bears profuse clusters of mauve-purple to white flowers up to 3 in (8 cm) wide. While needing a cool,

Abutilon × hybridum 'Orange King'

Abutilon × hybridum 'Kentish Belle'

Abutilon vitifolium

Abutilon vitifolium 'Album'

moist climate, it is one of the most cold-hardy abutilons, but does best against a sheltered wall or in a court-yard. Prune hard in early spring to prevent the shrub becoming straggly. Named cultivars include '**Veronica Tennant**', with fine, very pale laven-der flowers; and '**Album**', with white flowers. ZONES 8–9.

ANDROMEDA

Bog rosemary

Only 2 species of low evergreen shrubs make up this genus from the colder parts of the Northern Hemisphere. They have tough, short branches that root along the ground and small, oblong, leathery leaves. The small flowers, in short terminal sprays, are urn-shaped with a narrow aperture. CULTIVATION These shrubs are best grown in a shaded rockery. They prefer moist yet well-drained,

acid soil. They tolerate heavy frost and prefer a cold climate. Propagate either from seed or small tip cuttings.

Andromeda polifolia

Growing to about 24 in (60 cm) high and wide, this species has nar-row, deep green, 1 in (25 mm) long leaves with pale undersides. The tiny white to pink flowers appear in sprays in spring. '**Compacta**' has a denser, more compact habit, with grayish leaves and pink flowers. ZONES 2–9.

Andromeda polifolia

ARGYRANTHEMUM

Marguerite

One of several horticulturally important genera now recognized in place of the once more broadly defined *Chrysanthemum*, this genus consists of 22 species of evergreen subshrubs from the Canary Islands and Madeira. They tend to be upright, rarely over 3 ft (1 m) tall, and bushy with deeply lobed or divided, bright green to blue-green foliage. From spring to autumn in cool climates, and generally in winter–spring in warmer climates, the bushes are covered in 1–3 in (2.5–8 cm) wide daisies in white and a wide range of pink and yellow shades. Marguerites make good cut flowers and large numbers are sold potted by florists. In recent years, there has been a renewed interest in breeding, resulting in many new, exciting cultivars.

CULTIVATION Marguerites are very easy to cultivate in any light, well-drained soil in full sun. They grow particularly well near the sea and have naturalized in some coastal areas of the world. They should be cut back either in late winter or late summer to encourage fresh growth. Most species and cultivars tolerate light, irregular frosts only. Propagate either from seed or cuttings.

Argyranthemum frutescens

Argyranthemum frutescens
syn. *Chrysanthemum frutescens*

Although the true species, a 3 ft (1 m) tall, white-flowered shrub from the Canary Islands, is now rarely cultivated, most of the commonly seen garden cultivars are classified under this name, though many may in fact be hybrids with other species. There are numerous cultivars with a huge range of flower forms and sizes in a range of colors from white to deep pink and yellow. Some notable

Argyranthemum frutescens 'Bridesmaid'

Argyranthemum frutescens 'California Gold'

Argyranthemum frutescens 'Weymouth Pink'

examples include: **'Bridesmaid'**, **'California Gold'**, **'Harvest Gold'**,

Argyranthemum frutescens 'Margaret'

Argyranthemum frutescens 'Rising Sun'

'Jamaica Primrose', **'Little Rex'**, **'Margaret'**, **'Pink Lady'**, **'Rising Sun'**, **'Silver Leaf'**, **'Snow Man'**, **'Tauranga Star'** and **'Weymouth Pink'**. Provide winter protection. They also grow well in hanging baskets. ZONES 8–11.

BERBERIS

Barberry

This is a large genus of well over 400 species of hardy shrubs, both evergreen and deciduous, mostly branching from below the ground into densely massed canes and with weak to quite fierce spines where the leaves join the stems. The leaves are generally rather leathery, of small to medium size and often with prickly, marginal teeth. Clusters of small, yellow, cream, orange or reddish flowers are followed by small fleshy fruits. Most *Berberis* species come from

Berberis × *ottawensis* 'Superba'

Berberis × *ottawensis* 'Superba'

temperate East Asia, a few from Europe, and several from Andean South America. North American species once placed in *Berberis* are now referred to *Mahonia*.

CULTIVATION Barberries are easy to grow and thrive in most soil types. Withstanding hard pruning, they are useful for hedges. Propagate from seed or cuttings. In some countries there are restrictions on cultivating barberries because some species can harbor the overwintering phase of the wheat rust fungus.

Berberis × *ottawensis*

This hybrid is best known in the form of the clone '**Superba**' (syn. 'Purpurea'), which is similar to and often confused with B. *thunbergii* 'Atropurpurea', but is taller, around 6 ft (1.8 m), and more vigorous, with the new growths bronze red rather than dark purplish. Its red berries appear in autumn. It is a popular and very hardy deciduous shrub with densely massed stems, useful for hedging or to provide contrast among green-leafed shrubs. It is also prized by flower arrangers. ZONES 3–10.

Berberis thunbergii
Thunberg barberry, Japanese barberry

This is one of the most extensively planted barberries, usually in the guise of one of its cultivars. Native to Japan, it is a low-growing

Useful Tip

Delay pruning tender shrubs until after winter. The damaged growth may look unsightly but it can help protect the healthy parts.

Berberis thunbergii 'Red Pillar'

deciduous shrub (almost evergreen in warmer climates) growing about 5 ft (1.5 m) in height, with densely massed stems and small, neatly rounded leaves. Its spines are not particularly fierce. The small, bell-shaped flowers that appear in mid-spring are greenish yellow with dull red stripes. 'Atropurpurea' has deep purplish brown foliage turning a metallic bronze-black in late autumn. 'Atropurpurea Nana' (syn. 'Crimson Pygmy', 'Little Favorite') is a neat, bun-shaped plant only 12–18 in (30–45 cm) high, with similar toning plus green tints. 'Keller's Surprise' is compact and rather narrow, with green or bronze leaves splashed with pink. 'Rose Glow' has rich purple leaves, variously marked with pink, with green margins. 'Red Pillar'

is an improved form of the earlier cultivar 'Erecta' and has purple-red foliage and a very upright growth habit to around 4–5 ft (1.2–1.5 m) tall. ZONES 4–10.

BRACHYGLOTTIS

This genus of low evergreen shrubs and small trees contains about 30 species. Most are New Zealand natives, but one or two occur in Tasmania. Apart from their flowers, many are valued for their attract-ive foliage. The flowerheads are in small to rather large panicles at the branch tips, and may either be white or golden yellow with conspicuous petals (actually ray florets), or small and greenish white with no ray florets.

Brachyglottis, Dunedin Hybrid, 'Sunshine'

CULTIVATION These are rewarding garden plants in a suitable climate—they do best in cool but mild and rainy climates, in a sunny position with well-drained soil. The shrubby species respond well to heavy pruning. Propagate from cuttings in late summer. Keep them in shape by cutting back.

Brachyglottis, Dunedin Hybrids

Of mixed parentage involving three species, the Dunedin Hybrids are the result of a chance crossing early in the twentieth century at Dunedin in New Zealand. They are bushy, if somewhat open, shrubs to 5 ft (1.5 m) tall; their dark green leaves have the felty, white undersurface characteristic of the genus, and they bear daisy-like yellow flowerheads. 'Sunshine' has neat elliptical leaves and bright yellow flowerheads in large, loose terminal clusters. ZONES 7–9.

BUDDLEJA

Often spelt Buddleia, after the seventeenth-century English botanist Adam Buddle, *Buddleja* is now ruled the correct form. This genus consists of shrubs and small, mostly short-lived trees, both evergreen and deciduous. Most of the cultivated species originate in China, but the genus

Buddleja alternifolia

also occurs elsewhere, and includes many tropical and subtropical species. The leaves, usually in opposite pairs, are large, pointed and often crepe-textured. The spice-scented flowers are small and tubular, and appear in dense spikes at the branch tips, or sometimes in smaller clusters along the branches. They range through pinks, mauves, reddish purples, oranges and yellows.

CULTIVATION Buddlejas prefer full sun and good drainage, but thrive in any soil type. Fairly hard pruning in early spring controls their straggly appearance. Propagate from cuttings in summer.

Buddleja alternifolia

In full bloom in late spring and early summer, this tall deciduous shrub from northwestern China is transformed into a fountain of fragrant, mauve-pink blossom, the small individual flowers strung in clusters along its arching branches. It looks best trained to a single trunk so the branches can weep effectively. It should not be pruned back hard as it flowers on the previous summer's wood. ZONES 6–9.

Buddleja davidii
Butterfly bush

The common buddleja of gardens, *Buddleja davidii* is native to central

Buddleja davidii 'Cardinal'

Buddleja davidii 'Royal Red'

and western China. It is a decidu-ous or semi-evergreen shrub about 12 ft (3.5 m) tall, with gray-green foliage. In late summer and early autumn its arching canes bear at their tips long, narrow cones of densely packed flowers, mauve with an orange eye in the original form. These are attractive to butterflies, which feed on the scented nectar.

Prune in late winter to encourage strong canes with larger flower spikes. Cultivars with flowers in larger spikes and richer tones include 'Cardinal', rich purple-pink; 'Black Knight', dark purple; 'Empire Blue', purple-blue with an orange eye; 'Royal Red', magenta; and 'White Bouquet', cream with an orange eye. 'Dubonnet' has large

Buddleja davidii 'Dubonnet'

Buddleja davidii 'Pink Delight'

spikes of purple-pink flowers, and **'Pink Delight'** has long narrow spikes of bright pink blooms. The flowers of **'White Profusion'** are white with golden yellow centers. ZONES 5–10.

C

CALLISTEMON

Bottlebrush

These evergreen Australian shrubs and small trees bear magnificent long-stamened, mostly red flowers in dense, cylindrical spikes. The tips of the flower spikes continue to grow as leafy shoots, leaving long-lasting, woody seed capsules that eventually become half embedded in the thickening branch. Many species feature a weeping habit and a few have a striking papery bark, like that in the related genus *Melaleuca*. The 25 species hybridize freely and seed from mixed stands cannot be trusted to come true. In recent decades, many hybrid cultivars have been named, most of uncertain parentage, with flowers in a variety of hues in the white, pink to red range.

CULTIVATION The shrubby callistemons make a fine addition to the shrub border, where they attract birds. In general, they are only marginally frost tolerant and prefer full sun and moist soil; some, however, will tolerate poor drainage. A light pruning after flowering will prevent seed capsules forming and helps promote bushiness and flowering. Prune to make a single trunk on tree-like species. Propagate species from seed, cultivars and selected clones from tip cuttings.

Callistemon citrinus
syn. *Callistemon lanceolatus*
Scarlet bottlebrush, lemon bottlebrush

Widely distributed through coastal southeastern Australia, this stiff-leafed, bushy shrub was among the first bottlebrushes to be taken into cultivation. Its botanical epithet refers to a lemon scent in the crushed leaves, but this is barely detectable.

Useful Tip

Many tender shrubs can be espaliered against a wall where they benefit from the extra shelter.

Callistemon citrinus 'Burgundy'

A tough and vigorous plant with a short basal trunk, it usually grows quite rapidly to 10 ft (3 m), but may remain at much the same size for many years. The scarlet to crimson spikes, 4 in (10 cm) long and held erect, appear in late spring and summer, often with an autumn flush as well. A variable species, it has a number of wild races as well as many cultivars, including '**Burgundy**', with clustered, wine-colored brushes and attractive pinkish red leaves when young; '**Mauve Mist**',

Callistemon citrinus 'Reeves Pink'

also with colored new leaves and abundant brushes are mauve on opening and age to a deeper magenta; **'Reeves Pink'**, a denser shrub with clear pink flowers; **'Splendens'** (syn. 'Endeavour'), an early cultivar making a compact bush bearing bright scarlet brushes over a long period; and **'White Anzac'** (syn. 'Albus'), with white flowers. Protect from winter frosts. It also makes a most attractive potted plant.
ZONES 8–11.

Callistemon citrinus 'Splendens'

CALLUNA

Heather, ling

The single species of this genus, heather, is an evergreen shrub and is the dominant moorland plant of the colder parts of the UK and northern Europe; it is closely related to the heath genus *Erica*. White, pink, red or purple are the usual colors for the small, bell-shaped flowers, borne in dense clusters. In winter the foliage turns brownish or dull purple. Mostly grown in gardens are the numerous cultivars, selected for dwarf or compact growth and for flower or foliage color.
CULTIVATION It is an extremely frost-hardy plant, thriving in very exposed situations and often performing poorly under kinder conditions. The soil should be acidic, gritty, and of low fertility. After flowering, cut back to keep bushes compact. In regions with warm, humid summers it is prone to root- and stem-rot. Propagation is usually from tip cuttings or rooted branches can be detached.

Calluna vulgaris

Common heather makes a spreading shrub 12–36 in (30–90 cm) high. The flowers of wild plants are pale pink to a strong purplish pink, occasionally white. Flowering time is variable: some races and cultivars flower through summer, others from midsummer to early autumn. With over 400 cultivars available, it is hard to decide which to mention, but the following are representative and will add interest

Calluna vulgaris 'H. E. Beale'

and diversity to the garden. '**H. E. Beale**' is quite a tall specimen, to 30 in (75 cm), with grayish green foliage and long racemes of silvery pink double flowers held late in the season. '**Multicolor**', 4 in (10 cm) tall with a 10 in (25 cm) spread, is a compact variety with interesting yellow-green foliage tinged orange and red with racemes of mauve

blooms. '**Orange Queen**' is a very compact plant grown for its foliage: golden yellow in summer, changing to deep burnt-orange in winter; it has single pink flowers. ZONES 4–9.

CALYCANTHUS

Allspice

Only 2 or 3 species make up this genus of deciduous, cool-climate shrubs from North America. The leaves, bark and wood all have a spicy aroma when they are cut or bruised. They are grown for their curiously colored flowers, which appear singly among the leaves in late spring or summer and resemble small magnolia flowers

Useful Tip

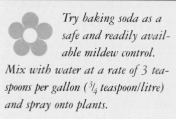

Try baking soda as a safe and readily available mildew control.
Mix with water at a rate of 3 teaspoons per gallon (³/₄ teaspoon/litre) and spray onto plants.

with narrow petals that are deep red-brown or dull reddish purple. The flowers make interesting indoor decorations.

CULTIVATION Undemanding shrubs, they flower best in a sunny but sheltered position in fertile, humus-rich, moist soil. Propagation is usually by layering branches, or from the seeds which are contained in soft, fig-like fruits.

Calycanthus floridus
Carolina allspice, sweet shrub

This shrub from southeastern USA grows 6–9 ft (1.8–2.7 m) tall and has broad, glossy, pale green leaves with downy undersides. Its 2 in (5 cm) wide, early summer flowers consist of many petals that are dull brownish red, often with paler tips. ZONES 6–10.

Calycanthus floridus

CAMELLIA

Camellias are among the most popular of flowering shrubs and a profusion of beautiful garden varieties has been produced. In the wild they are restricted to eastern Asia, ranging from Japan through southern and central China, with a few outliers in the eastern Himalayas and the Malay Archipelago. All species are evergreen shrubs or small trees. Their flower is always in the white-pink-red range, except for a small group of Vietnamese and Chinese species that have pale yellow to bronze-yellow flowers. Apart from the ornamental species, there are several camellias with economic importance of another kind. Tea is made from the dried and cured young leaves of *Camellia sinensis*. Plantations of *C. oleifera* are grown in its native southern China for the valuable oil pressed from its seeds, used in cooking and cosmetics. Several other species are also grown for their oil.

CULTIVATION Most camellias grow best in mild, humid climates and some species are very frost tender, but most of the cultivars are moderately frost hardy. They prefer well-drained, slightly acidic soil enriched with organic

Camellia japonica

matter and generally grow best in part-shade, though some cultivars are quite sun tolerant. Good drainage is important to prevent phytophthora root rot, but they like to be kept moist. Many varieties are suited to pot culture and make handsome tub specimens. Pruning is largely unnecessary, but trim them after flowering or cut back harder if rejuvenation is required. Propagate from cuttings in late summer or winter, or by grafting.

Useful Tip

If you cut roses for indoors, try adding some sugary (non-diet) soft drink to your vase water to prolong the flowers' life.

Camellia japonica

Wild plants of this best known *Camellia* species are small, scraggy trees 20–30 ft (6–9 m) tall in their

Camellia japonica 'Adolphe Audusson'

Camellia japonica 'Betty Sheffield Pink'

natural habitats, usually with red, somewhat funnel-shaped, 5-petaled flowers 2–3 in (5–8 cm) across. It is the cultivars of pure *Camellia japonica* origin that are seen in gardens, and so numerous are they, that *Camellia* enthusiasts have devised classifications of the cultivars based on flower size and form. Among representative cultivars, some old favorites are '**Adolphe Audusson**', with large, saucer-shaped, semi-double, dark red flowers sometimes with white markings and prominent yellow stamens; '**Chandleri**' is a bright red, anemone-form double of medium size; '**Magnoliiflora**' (syn. 'Hagoromo') has elegant semi-double, blush-pink blooms of medium size; '**Virginia Franco Rosea**' is a small formal double with many-rowed petals in soft pink with faint lines. Significant newer cultivars include '**Betty Sheffield Pink**', a medium-large incomplete double anemone-form, with wavy, pink petals sometimes irregularly splashed white; '**Guilio Nuccio**', a very large semi-double with very broad, irregular coral-red petals and prominent yellow stamens; '**Desire**', a medium-large formal double with pale pink shading to darker pink or lilac on the outside; '**Erin Farmer**', a large

Camellia japonica 'Guilio Nuccio'

Camellia japonica 'Desire'

Camellia japonica 'Bokuhan'

semi-double in orchid pink shading to almost white with golden stamens in the center. The best known miniature is **'Bokuhan'** (syn. 'Tinsie'); its tiny flowers have a ring of dark red petals surrounding a white bulb of petaloids. A fine Higo cultivar is **'Yamato Nishiki'** (syn. 'Brocade of Old Japan'), with large, single, white flowers broadly streaked pink and red, and a very wide circle of gold stamens. Representing a group of cultivars with curious foliage is

Camellia japonica 'Erin Farmer'

'Kingyo-Tsubaki' (syn. 'Fishtail', 'Mermaid'), with leaves mostly 3-lobed; the flowers are medium-small, single and rose pink. *C. japonica* cultivars vary in flowering time from late autumn to early spring in mild climates, and from early to late spring in cooler climates. They will not survive outdoors where winter temperatures drop much below 15°F (minus 10°C).
ZONES 5–10.

Camellia reticulata

Camellia reticulata makes a more upright plant than *C. japonica,* with an open framework of sparser foliage and large, leathery leaves. They are late blooming for camellias, flowering from late winter to midspring. The wild form sold as **Wild Type** has rather irregularly cup-shaped, single, reddish pink flowers about 3 in (8 cm) wide. The original introduction from 1820, **'Captain**

Camellia reticulata

Rawes', is still admired, with 6 in (15 cm) semi-double blooms of rich carmine-pink. Newer cultivars are more compact, for example, **'Lila Naff'**, a single, but with multiple broad petals of a most delicate pink, and **'William Hertrich'**, a very large semi-double with deep red petals. Many cultivars that are usually treated as reticulatas are in fact hybrids, with influence from other species. ZONES 8–10.

Camellia sasanqua

Originating in southern Japan, this small-leafed species has given rise to many hundreds of cultivars. The most versatile camellias from the landscaping point of view, the sasanquas have increased in popularity recently. They are densely

Camellia reticulata 'William Hertrich'

Camellia sasanqua

Different cultivars extend the flowering season from early autumn to midwinter. Sasanquas are faster growing and more sun tolerant than most camellias, performing better in mild climates. Among superior cultivars are 'Jennifer Susan', with clear pink, semi-double flowers; 'Plantation Pink', with large single, saucer-shaped, soft pink flowers, is excellent for hedging; 'Paradise Belinda' is a semi-double with the outer stamens bearing small petal-like organs, giving it an unusual effect; and 'Mine-no-yuki' (syn. 'White Doves'), a creamy semi-double that can be successfully espaliered. ZONES 8–11.

leafed plants that can be grown as hedges, and some cultivars are suited to espaliering against a wall or fence. They have small, shiny, dark green leaves and small to medium-sized, delicately fragrant, mostly single or semi-double flowers in a variety of colors. Flowering is profuse but individual flowers are short lived.

Camellia × williamsii

Although hybrid camellias are dealt with separately, this group is so well known it merits its own heading. All these hybrids are crosses between *Camellia japonica* and the western

Camellia sasanqua 'Plantation Pink'

Camellia sasanqua 'Paradise Belinda'

Camellia × *williamsii* 'Donation'

Camellia × *williamsii* 'E. G. Waterhouse'

Chinese high altitude species *C. saluenensis*, or seedlings of succeeding generations. Much of their popularity is due to their cold hardiness and profuse blooms in clear colors, borne over a long winter and spring season. One of the earliest and best known is **'Donation'**, with large, orchid pink, semi-double flowers. **'Caerhays'** has medium-sized, semi-double, lilac-rose flowers on somewhat pendulous branches. **'E. G. Waterhouse'** has an erect habit, matt green foliage and formal double flowers of a rich fuchsia pink. ZONES 7–10.

Camellia × *williamsii* 'Donation'

Camellia Hybrid 'Brian'

Camellia Hybrids

The most widely used parents of *Camellia* Hybrids are *C. japonica, C. sasanqua* and *C. reticulata*, but many others have also been used, including some of the small-flowered species such as *C. tsaii*. In this way, the diversity of foliage, flower and growth form is extended; the addition of fragrance to camellia blooms is one direction breeders are taking. Some representative cultivars are **'Brian'**, which has rose pink pointed petals

Camellia Hybrid 'Cornish Snow'

in a hose-in-hose arrangement up to 4 in (10 cm) across, and a vigorous, upright habit; the very cold-hardy **'Cornish Snow'**, with profuse, delicate, small, single white flowers sometimes flushed pink, and a tall, open habit; **'Scentuous'**, a semi-double with white petals flushed pink on the reverse, an open habit and bright green leaves. **'Baby Bear'** is a small-flowered dwarf form, with light pink blooms and a dense habit ideal for bonsai or rockery use. ZONES 5–10.

CARPENTERIA

Bush anemone, tree anemone

Carpenteria californica is the only species belonging in this genus. It is an evergreen shrub with pure white flowers, like those of *Philadelphus*, but with 5 to 7 petals rather than 4, and a more conspicuous cluster of golden stamens. The leaves, arranged in opposite pairs on the soft-wooded branches, are narrow, soft and deep green above with paler green, felty undersides. It is a beautiful shrub when it blooms in late spring and early summer. This genus should not be confused with the palm genus *Carpentaria*.
CULTIVATION Although requiring a fairly cool climate, the bush anemone only flowers well in

regions with warm, dry summers. It needs ample sunshine, well-drained, gritty soil that must not dry out too much, and protection from strong winds. Propagation is usually from seed, as cuttings do not root easily.

Carpenteria californica

In the wild, this very attractive shrub grows only in a small area of central California, on dry mountain slopes. It can grow to 20 ft (6 m) tall, but in gardens it is usually a sprawling shrub 6–8 ft (1.8–2.4 m) tall. It may need support, so it is best grown against a sunny wall. The flowers, borne singly or in small groups, are normally 2–2½ in (5–6 cm) wide, but may be up to 4 in (10 cm) wide, with broadly overlapping petals. ZONES 7–9.

CARYOPTERIS

Bluebeard

This is a genus of 6 species of deciduous, erect subshrubs or woody perennials in the verbena family, all native to eastern Asia. They have slender, cane-like stems with thin, toothed leaves arranged in opposite pairs, and bear small blue or purple flowers in dense, stalked clusters in the leaf axils. Only 2 species have been grown much in gardens and even these are now largely replaced by the hybrid between them, represented by a number of cultivars. CULTIVATION These plants are often included in shrub borders where their grayish foliage and white or blue flowers blend well with plants of more robust color.

Carpenteria californica

Caryopteris × clandonensis

Caryopteris × clandonensis

They need to be placed in full sun and well-drained, humus-rich soil. Cut well back in early spring to ensure a good framework for the new season's growth and consequent late summer to autumn flowering. Seed can be used for propagation, but in the case of the many cultivars it is necessary to take soft-tip or semi-ripe cuttings.

Caryopteris × clandonensis
Hybrid bluebeard, blue-mist shrub

This subshrub, a cross between *Caryopteris incana* and *C. mongolica*, is prized for its masses of delicate, purple-blue flowers borne from late summer to autumn. It grows to a height and spread of 3 ft (1 m), and the oval leaves are gray-green and irregularly serrated. 'Ferndown', with dark violet-blue flowers, is a popular choice among the many cultivars. 'Heavenly Blue' has blooms of deep blue and 'Kew Blue' has darker green leaves and dark blue flowers. ZONES 5–9.

Caryopteris × clandonensis 'Ferndown'

CEANOTHUS

California lilac

Brilliant displays of blue, violet, or occasionally pink or white flowers are the chief attraction of most of the 50 or more species in this genus. Comprising evergreen and deciduous shrubs (some reaching small tree size), all of them are North American, with the vast majority confined to the coastal ranges of California. Some species that grow on coastal cliffs develop dense, prostrate forms highly resistant to salt spray. The leaves are small to medium sized, blunt tipped and usually toothed. The flowers, individually tiny with thread-like stalks, are massed in dense clusters at the ends of the branches; they appear in spring in most species.

CULTIVATION As garden plants, these shrubs can be outstandingly ornamental but are often short-lived, and are especially prone to sudden death in climates with warm, wet summers. They require full sun and prefer shelter, particularly from strong winds, in well-drained soil. Propagate from seed, often freely produced in small round capsules, or from cuttings.

Ceanothus × delilianus

This old French hybrid is a sturdy, vigorous, deciduous shrub with mid-

Ceanothus × delilianus 'Gloire de Versailles'

green leaves that are broad and oval. It originated as a cross between the New Jersey tea *(Ceanothus americanus)* of eastern USA and the tropical *C. coeruleus* from Mexico and Guatemala, which has sky blue flowers in large sprays. There are a number of fine cultivars, the best known being '**Gloire de Versailles**', a 12 ft (3.5 m) shrub with erect, loose panicles of pale blue, scented flowers from midsummer to early autumn. ZONES 7–9.

Useful Tip

Rhododendrons develop flower buds from early autumn so prune them in summer to avoid removing any buds.

Ceanothus impressus

Ceanothus impressus
Santa Barbara ceanothus

A free-flowering, small-leafed, evergreen species of dense, spreading habit, this is a first-class garden shrub under suitable conditions. The leaves are about $\frac{1}{2}$ in (12 mm) long and very thick and the veins

Ceanothus impressus 'Puget Blue'

are deeply impressed into the upper surface. In spring, it produces a profuse display of small clusters of deep blue flowers. From 6 to 10 ft (1.8 to 3 m) in height, this coastal Californian species prefers tough, exposed conditions. **'Puget Blue'** features stunning blue flowers and is probably a hybrid with *Ceanothus papillosus*. ZONES 8–10.

CHAENOMELES

Flowering quince

Related to *Cydonia* (the edible quince), with similar large, hard fruits, these many-stemmed deciduous shrubs bear red, pink or white flowers on a tangle of bare branches in early spring or even late winter. Originating in China, Japan and Korea, they are very frost hardy and adaptable. The tough, springy branches are often thorny on vigorous shoots; the leaves are simple and finely toothed. The flowers appear in stalkless clusters on the previous year's wood, followed in summer by yellow-green fruits with waxy, strongly perfumed skins that make fine jams and jellies. The wild forms have been superseded by a large selection of cultivars.

CULTIVATION *Chaenomeles* species do best in a sunny spot in well-drained, but not too rich, soil and

Chaenomeles speciosa 'Apple Blossom'

a dry atmosphere. Prune hard each year. Propagate from cuttings.

Chaenomeles speciosa
Chinese flowering quince, japonica

This species and its hybrids are the most commonly grown flowering quinces. Growing 5–10 ft (1.5–3 m) high, they spread by basal suckers to form dense thickets of stems. Their leaves are larger than those of *Chaenomeles japonica*, up to 4 in (10 cm) long and 1½ in (35 mm) wide, and the scarlet to deep red flowers, opening from late winter to midspring, are also larger. Modern cultivars vary in availability, but several older ones still widely grown include: **'Apple Blossom'**, white, flushed pink; **'Nivalis'**, white;

Chaenomeles speciosa 'Moerloosii'

'**Moerloosii**' is white, flushed and blotched pink and carmine; and the crimson '**Rubra Grandiflora**'. ZONES 6–10.

Chaenomeles × superba

This is a hybrid between *Chaenomeles japonica* and *C. speciosa,* with a height about midway between that of the two parents. It has given rise to a number of first-class cultivars like '**Knap Hill Scarlet**', with bright orange-scarlet flowers; '**Crimson and Gold**', with deep crimson petals and gold anthers; '**Nicoline**', with a rather sprawling habit and scarlet

Chaenomeles × superba

flowers; '**Pink Lady**', with large, bright rose-pink flowers; and '**Rowallane**', with blood-crimson flowers. ZONES 6–10.

CHAMAECYTISUS

A broom genus which consists of about 30 species of deciduous and evergreen shrubs from the Mediterranean region and the Canary Islands, *Chamaecytisus* is closely related to *Cytisus*, and its species were formerly included in the latter genus. They range from dwarf to quite tall shrubs; all have leaves consisting of 3 leaflets and produce clusters of white, yellow, pink or purple pea-flowers. Some are handsome rock-garden subjects, while at least one taller species is grown as a green manure plant and as fodder for animals.

CULTIVATION The smaller species should be grown in full sun in very well-drained soil, preferably in a raised position such as a rock garden. They are intolerant of transplanting. The taller species are less fussy and will grow in most soils and in a range of situations. Propagate from seed or cuttings.

Chamaecytisus purpureus
syn. *Cytisus purpureus*
Purple broom

Native to southeastern Europe, this is a low-growing, deciduous shrub reaching a height of about 18 in (45 cm), with a broadly spreading habit. Showy, lilac-purple flowers, about ³/₄ in (18 mm) long, appear

Chamaecytisus purpureus

Choisya ternata

in late spring and early summer, in clusters of 1 to 3 at each leaf axil. Flowering in the following season

is promoted by cutting back as soon as flowering has finished.
ZONES 6–9.

CHOISYA

This genus of 8 species of evergreen shrubs belongs to the same family as citrus, and is from Mexico and the far south of the USA. One species is widely cultivated as an ornamental in warm-temperate climates. Their leaves are compound, with 3 to 7 leaflets radiating from the stalk apex; from the leaf axils arise clusters of

Choisya ternata 'Sundance'

fragrant, star-shaped, white flowers, resembling orange-blossoms. The crushed or bruised leaves are also aromatic.

CULTIVATION *Choisya* make excellent hedging plants as well as being attractive additions to borders, growing best in full sun or part shade and in slightly acid, humus-rich, well-drained soil. Protect from strong winds, fertilize in spring, and trim lightly after flowering to keep the foliage dense and ground-hugging. Propagate from tip cuttings in autumn.

Choisya ternata
Mexican orange blossom

One of the most frost-hardy evergreens to come from the highlands of Mexico, this popular species makes a compact, rounded bush to 6 ft (1.8 m) or more. Its attractive leaves consist of 3 glossy, deep green leaflets. Tight clusters of small,

white, fragrant flowers appear among the leaves in spring, and sometimes again in late summer. The cultivar 'Sundance' has golden yellow foliage when young, maturing to yellow-green. ZONES 7–11.

CISTUS

Rock rose

These evergreen shrubs, from around the Mediterranean and the Canary Islands, are valued for their attractive, saucer-shaped flowers with crinkled petals in shades of pink, purple or white and a central boss of golden stamens, like a single rose. Although short-lived, most bloom over a long season, some for almost the whole year, and they do very well in borders, on banks or in pots; some examples include **'Peggy Sammons'**, **'Santa Cruz'**, **'Snow Mound'** and

Cistus 'Peggy Sammons'

Cistus 'Snow Mound'

Cistus 'Warley Rose'

'Warley Rose'. Some *Cistus* species exude an aromatic resin, which the Greeks and Romans called *labdanum* and used for incense and perfume, as well as for its alleged medicinal properties.

CULTIVATION These shrubs are easily cultivated, provided they are given a warm, sunny position and very well-drained, even rather dry, soil; they like being among large rocks or other rubble where their roots can seek out moisture. If necessary, they can be tip pruned to promote bushiness, or the main branches can be shortened by about one-third after flowering. Most species are moderately frost hardy; all are resistant to very dry conditions. They will thrive in cool- to warm-temperate climates, but not in subtropical regions with hot, humid summers. Propagate from cuttings; seed, although readily germinated, gives slower results.

Cistus ladanifer
Crimson-spot rock rose

The most upright and slender species, *Cistus ladanifer* grows 5–6 ft (1.5–1.8 m) tall, but then quickly becomes sparse and leggy and does not take well to pruning. The whole plant, apart from the flower petals, is coated with a shiny resin that in the heat of the day becomes semi-liquid and very aromatic. Its leaves

Cistus ladanifer

are narrow and dark green and the flowers, among the largest in the genus at 3–4 in (7–10 cm) in diameter, have white petals, each with a reddish chocolate basal blotch; they appear from midspring to early summer. The cultivar '**Albiflorus**' has pure white petals. ZONES 8–10.

Cistus ladanifer 'Albiflorus'

Cistus ladanifer 'Albiflorus'

Cistus × purpureus 'Brilliancy'

Cistus × purpureus
Orchid rock rose

This hybrid between *Cistus ladanifer* and *C. creticus* has deep pink flowers with prominent, dark reddish chocolate blotches on the petals. It is free flowering and frost hardy. Several clones have been named, including 'Brilliancy', with clear pink petals, and 'Betty Taudevin', a deeper reddish pink. ZONES 7–9.

CORYLOPSIS

Winter hazel

These deciduous shrubs from China and Japan produce short, usually pendulous spikes of fragrant, 5-petaled, pale yellow or greenish flowers on the bare branches, before the blunt-toothed leaves appear in late spring. The fruits, ripening in summer among the leaves, are small, woody capsules, each containing 2 black seeds. The appeal of these shrubs lies mostly in the repetitive pattern of flower spikes on the bare branches.

Corylopsis glabrescens

CULTIVATION Corylopsis species are best suited to a woodland setting in a reasonably moist, cool climate, providing a foil for bolder shrubs such as rhododendrons. The soil should be fertile, moist but well-drained and acid. Propagation is normally from seed.

Corylopsis glabrescens
Fragrant winter hazel

Native to Japan where it grows in the mountains, this attractive species makes a broadly spreading shrub of 15 ft (4.5 m) tall, sometimes even higher. The small flowers are lemon yellow with rather narrow petals and appear in midspring. ZONES 6–9.

COTINUS

Smoke bush, smoke tree

Only 3 species make up this genus of deciduous shrubs or small trees: one is from temperate Eurasia, one from eastern North America, and one is confined to southwestern China. They have simple, oval, untoothed leaves. A striking feature is the much-branched inflorescences, with delicate, thread-like dull purplish branchlets, only a few of which carry the small flowers; they produce a curiously ornamental effect like fine puffs of smoke scattered over the foliage. Both flowers and fruits are tiny

Cotinus coggygria 'Velvet Cloak'

and inconspicuous. The foliage is another attraction, coloring deeply in autumn, and in some cultivars the spring foliage offers a good display of rich color.

CULTIVATION Smoke bushes are easily grown, adapting to a range of temperate climates, but they are most at home where the summers are moderately warm and dry. Soil that is too moist or fertile discourages free flowering. Propagate from softwood cuttings in summer or seed in autumn.

Useful Tip

Make your flowering shrubs do double duty after flowering: berrying branches last just as well, if not better, than flowers if cut and kept in water.

Cotinus coggygria 'Purpureus'

Cotinus coggygria
syn. *Rhus cotinus*
Venetian sumac, smoke tree

Of wide distribution from southern Europe to central China, this bushy shrub is usually 10–15 ft (3–4 m) in height and spread, and has oval, long-stalked leaves. The inflorescences appear in early summer and are pale pinkish bronze, ageing to a duller purple-gray. Some of the flowers produce small, dry, flattened fruit in late summer. The autumn foliage has strong orange and bronze tones. '**Purpureus**', a widely grown cultivar, has rich, purplish spring foliage, which becomes greener in summer and glowing orange and purple in autumn; '**Royal Purple**' is very similar but the spring and summer foliage is a deeper purple; the leaves of '**Velvet Cloak**' are purple and turn dark reddish purple in autumn. ZONES 6–10.

Cotinus coggygria 'Royal Purple'

CYTISUS

Broom

The brooms are a diverse group of usually yellow-flowered, leguminous shrubs and subshrubs from Europe and the Mediterranean region, which include a number of genera—the most important are *Cytisus* and *Genista*. *Cytisus* is a variable genus, in habit ranging from tall and erect to prostrate. Some of the 30 species have well-developed leaves, either simple and narrow or composed of 3 leaflets, while others are almost leafless, with photosynthesis performed by the green, angled branchlets. All have pea-flowers in small, profuse clusters along new growth.

CULTIVATION Generally easy garden subjects, they flower well under most conditions except deep shade, tolerating both dry and boggy, fertile or quite infertile soils. Some smaller species demand warm, dry positions in a rock garden in pockets of well-drained soil. They are easily propagated from seed, cuttings or, in the case of some named cultivars, by grafting.

Cytisus scoparius 'Pendulus'

Cytisus × praecox
Warminster broom, moonlight broom

This hybrid between the tall *Cytisus multiflorus* and the lower-growing *C. purgans* includes several popular cultivars, all of them free-flowering shrubs of 3–4 ft (1–1.2 m) tall, with massed, slender branchlets arising from ground level and spreading gracefully. The original hybrid has cream and yellow flowers, with a heavy fragrance, borne in mid- to late spring. More recent cultivars include '**Allgold**', with cascading sprays of soft, golden yellow blossom, and '**Goldspear**', a lower and broader shrub with deeper gold flowers. ZONES 5–9.

Cytisus scoparius
Common broom, Scotch broom

Widely distributed in central and western Europe, including the UK, this is one of the taller and most vigorous species of *Cytisus*, reaching 6–8 ft (1.8–2.4 m) in height, and making a great show of golden yellow blossoms in late spring and early summer. The black seed pods may be abundant, ripening in mid-summer and scattering their seed with a sharp, cracking sound in hot, dry weather. In cooler areas of some Southern Hemisphere countries it has become a troublesome weed. '**Pendulus**' has pendulous branches. ZONES 5–9.

Cytisus × praecox 'Allgold'

D

DAPHNE

Daphne

Originating from Europe, North Africa and temperate Asia, this genus includes 50 or so deciduous and evergreen shrubs. They have simple, leathery leaves and small, highly fragrant flowers clustered at the shoot tips or leaf axils. Although the flower parts are not differentiated into true petals and sepals—for the sake of simplicity here they are called "petals"—of which there are always four, characteristically pointed, recurving and rather fleshy. In the wild, many daphnes occur on mountains in stony ground, often on limestone. CULTIVATION Daphnes prefer cool, well-aerated, gritty, humusrich soil. They are intolerant of root disturbance, and are best planted out while small. The taller species are better adapted to sheltered woodlands, the smaller ones to rock gardens. Propagate either from cuttings or layers. Fresh seed usually germinates readily but many species fail to fruit.

Daphne bholua

This species, from the eastern Himalayas, can be evergreen or deciduous depending on the form selected. It usually grows into an upright shrub up to 12 ft (3.5 m) tall and 5 ft (1.5 m) wide. It bears clusters of highly scented, soft pink flowers in late winter. Selected

Daphne bholua 'Gurkha'

Daphne bholua 'Jacqueline Postill'

forms include **'Gurkha'**, which is deciduous, and **'Jacqueline Postill'**, which is evergreen. ZONES 6–9.

Daphne × burkwoodii

This is a most attractive, rounded, semi-evergreen shrub up to 3 ft (1 m) tall. Its pale pink flowers, darker in bud, appear in mid- to late spring, sometimes through summer. The most easily grown deciduous daphne, it flowers best in full sun. 'Somerset' is slightly more vigorous and has deep pink flowers with pale pink lobes. ZONES 5–9.

Daphne cneorum

Garland flower, rose daphne

This low growing, to 16 in (40 cm), evergreen shrub from southern Europe has a loose, semi-prostrate habit, with trailing main shoots and dense lateral branches. It has

Daphne × burkwoodii

Daphne × burkwoodii 'Somerset'

small, dark green leaves and bears fragrant, rose-pink flowers in mid-spring. It is a sun-loving plant but requires moist, well-drained soil. ZONES 4–9.

Daphne genkwa
Lilac daphne

Indigenous to China but long culti-vated in Japan, this small deciduous shrub tends to be short lived in cultivation. It is sparsely branched, producing long, wiry growths in summer which, the following spring, while still leafless, bear clusters of delicate, long-tubed, lilac flowers at every leaf axil. It prefers sheltered, sunny, frost-free conditions. ZONES 5–9.

Daphne odora
syn. *Daphne indica*
Winter daphne

A Chinese evergreen shrub long cultivated in Japan, *Daphne odora* is

Daphne cneorum

a spreading, twiggy shrub to 4 ft (1.2 m) in height, with dark green leaves. From late autumn to midspring its rose-purple buds open to almost pure white, waxy

Daphne genkwa

Daphne odora

flowers. The cultivar '**Alba**' is pure white, and '**Aureomarginata**' has yellow-edged leaves and flowers marked reddish purple. ZONES 8–10.

DEUTZIA

These summer-flowering, deciduous shrubs from East Asia and the Himalayas are closely related to *Philadelphus* but their smaller white or pink flowers have 5, rather than 4, pointed petals, and are borne in more crowded sprays. Like *Philadelphus,* the plants have long, straight, cane-like stems. The leaves occur in opposite pairs and are mostly finely toothed. There are many frost-hardy species and fine hybrids available, particularly those bred by the Lémoine nursery at Nancy, France, from 1890 to 1940.

CULTIVATION Deutzias prefer a sheltered position, moist fertile soil and some sun during the day. Avoid pruning the previous year's short lateral shoots; thin out canes and shorten some of the thickest old stems after flowering. Propagate from seed or cuttings taken in late spring.

Deutzia crenata var. *nakaiana* 'Nikko'

Deutzia crenata var. nakaiana 'Nikko'

syn. *Deutzia gracilis* 'Nikko'

This, one of the smallest deutzias, makes a low spreading mound, often rooting as it spreads. It is a good rock-garden plant or ground cover in a shrub border, growing to about 24 in (60 cm) tall and as much as 4 ft (1.2 m) wide. The starry, white flowers are produced in spikes in summer and the pale green foliage turns reddish purple in autumn, before being shed. ZONES 5–9.

Deutzia × rosea

One of the earliest Lémoine crosses between *Deutzia gracilis* and *D. purpurascens*, it reaches a height and spread of 30 in (75 cm) and has the low, spreading habit of the former

Deutzia × *rosea* 'Carminea'

species with the pink coloration of the latter. The original clone has flowers of the palest pink, in shorter, broader sprays than in *D. gracilis*. 'Carminea' has larger panicles of pink flowers with a stronger carmine pink on the back. ZONES 5–9.

Deutzia × *rosea* 'Carminea'

Deutzia scabra

Deutzia scabra

This, the longest established and most robust species in Western gardens, has thick canes growing to about 10 ft (3 m), and long, dull green, rough-textured leaves. The large panicles of white, bell-shaped flowers terminate upper branches from midspring to early summer. **'Flore Pleno'** has double flowers, striped dull pink on the outside; **'Candidissima'** is a pure white double; and **'Pride of Rochester'**, another double, has larger flowers faintly tinted mauve outside. ZONES 5–10.

Deutzia scabra 'Pride of Rochester'

E

ECHIUM

Indigenous to the Mediterranean, Canary Islands and Madeira, the 40 or so species of annuals, perennials and shrubs in this genus are grown for their spectacular bright blue, purple or pink flowers that appear in late spring and summer. The hairy leaves form rosettes at the bases of the flowering stems. They look best in mixed borders. Ingestion of the plants can cause stomach upsets. **CULTIVATION** Very frost hardy to frost tender, *Echium* species do best in a dry climate, full sun and a light to medium, well-drained soil. They become unwieldy in soil that is too rich or damp. Prune gently after flowering to keep the plants compact. Coastal planting is ideal. Propagate from seed or cuttings in spring or summer. In mild climates they self-seed readily.

Echium candicans
syn. *Echium fastuosum*
Pride of Madeira, tower of jewels

This soft-wooded shrub has fuzzy, gray-green leaves, broadly sword-shaped and clustered in large rosettes at the branch ends. In spring and summer, 24 in (60 cm) spires of sapphire-blue to violet-blue flowers with reddish pink stamens are borne, each about ½ in (12 mm) wide but produced in hundreds together. Sprawling in habit, it grows to about 1.8 m (6 ft) tall but spreads wider. **ZONES 9–10.**

Echium candicans

ENKIANTHUS

About 10 species of deciduous shrubs from East Asia make up this genus. They are valued for their small, densely clustered, bell-shaped flowers and fine autumn foliage. Growth is rather open and the smallish leaves are clustered at the end of each season's growth, producing a layered effect. The stalked, pendulous flowers are produced in numerous short sprays.

CULTIVATION Very frost hardy, they like similar conditions to many rhododendrons and azaleas: moist woodland with humus-rich, but not too fertile, acid soil. They will not thrive in heavy shade. Avoid pruning to a rounded shape as the flowers will not be so well displayed. Propagate from seed or cuttings in summer.

Enkianthus perulatus
White enkianthus

This Japanese species is rather distinctive among enkianthuses in its lower, bushier habit and its sparser, urn-shaped flowers that are white or greenish white, without markings and contracted at the mouth. They are borne on nodding stalks in early spring. This species likes a very cool, sheltered position and has brilliant red autumn foliage. ZONES 6–9.

Enkianthus perulatus

ERICA

Heath

This large genus is made up of more than 800 species of small-leafed, free-flowering, evergreen shrubs. The vast majority is native to South Africa, but a relatively small number of species occur in Europe and elsewhere in Africa. In Europe, several *Erica* species, together with the closely related *Calluna* (heather), dominate moorland vegetation. The Cape heaths from South Africa, often with long, tubular flowers, are fine garden plants in mild-winter climates where summer humidity is low. The European species bear smaller, bell-shaped flowers in a more limited white to deep pink range but are frost hardy and are very popular garden plants.

CULTIVATION Most *Erica* species like full sun, well-drained, neutral to acid soil and dislike lime and animal manure. Prune after flowering to keep plants bushy and compact. Propagate from seed or from cuttings in late summer.

Erica carnea 'March Seedling'

Erica carnea
syn. *Erica herbacea*
Winter heath, snow heath

From the mountains of central and southern Europe, this frost-hardy species and its numerous cultivars are among the few heaths that will thrive in chalk soils. It forms a low, spreading subshrub, usually less than 12 in (30 cm) high, with densely crowded branches. Through most of winter and into early spring, it produces a fine display of small, urn-shaped, purple-pink flowers with protruding darker stamens. This is an ideal ground cover between taller shrubs or beneath deciduous trees, or in rock gardens. Well-known cultivars include '**December Red**', with purplish pink flowers and '**March Seedling**', which flowers until late spring. Others

Erica carnea 'Myretoun Ruby'

Erica carnea 'Springwood White'

are '**Myretoun Ruby**', with very dark green leaves against bright rose-pink flowers; '**Ruby Glow**', with deep rose-red flowers; '**Spring-wood Pink**', with a vigorous trailing habit and rose-pink flowers; and '**Springwood White**', with a spreading habit, vigorous growth and white flowers. ZONES 5–9.

Erica cinerea
Bell heather, twisted heath

Native throughout Western Europe, including the British Isles, this heather is one of the loveliest of the frost-hardy heaths. Its small, crowded, rose-pink bells are produced over a long season from early summer to early autumn. Low and spreading, the ends of the twisted branches ascend to 12–18 in (30–45 cm). Bell heather dislikes hot summer weather, which scorches its foliage and may kill the plant. The many named cultivars vary chiefly in flower color from white to rich rose purple; some also have golden or coppery foliage. '**Kerry Cherry**' has deep pink flowers; '**Crimson King**' is crimson; and '**Golden Drop**' has golden summer foliage with coppery tints, turning red in winter. ZONES 5–9.

Erica × darleyensis
Darley Dale heath

Erica × darleyensis is a hybrid of the two frost-hardy species, *E. erigena* and *E. carnea*, and has proved to be a valuable garden plant. It forms a dense, bushy shrub to 24 in (60 cm) high, with dark green foliage, and

Erica cinerea 'Kerry Cherry'

Erica cinerea 'Crimson King'

Erica × darleyensis

Erica × darleyensis 'Darley Dale'

from late autumn through spring is covered in crowded, short spikes of cylindrical, pale rose flowers with protruding, darker stamens. It tolerates chalk soils. The original clone is now known as **'Darley Dale'** but others, with flowers ranging from white to deep pink, are listed: **'Dunwood Splendour'** spreads widely and produces a spectacular display of mauve-pink flowers; **'George Rendall'** is a compact grower with purplish pink flowers throughout winter; **'Jack H. Brummage'** has golden to red-tinted winter foliage and purplish pink flowers; and **'White Perfection'** has bright green foliage and pure white flowers. ZONES 6–9.

Erica erigena
syn. *Erica hibernica, E. mediterranea*
Irish heath, Mediterranean heath

This western European species has deep green foliage and massed, urn-shaped, bright pink flowers in

Erica × darleyensis 'White Perfection'

Erica erigena 'Alba Compacta'

Erica erigena 'Hibernica'

winter and spring. It grows to 6 ft (1.8 m) high and 3 ft (1 m) wide. Cultivars include **'Alba Compacta'**, a compact, white-flowered form; **'Ewan Jones'**, a vigorous grower with mauve-pink flowers set against dark green leaves; **'Hibernica'**, with shell-pink flowers; and **'Hibernica Alba'**, a spectacular white-flowered form growing about 3 ft (1 m) tall. **'Irish Dusk'** has rose-pink flowers and gray-green leaves; **'Mrs. Parris Lavender'** is an upright form to 18 in (45 cm) tall, with mauve flowers; **'Mrs. Parris White'** is an albino form of 'Mrs. Parris Lavender'; **'Silver Bells'** has white, scented flowers; **'Superba'** has pale pink, perfumed flowers; and **'W. T. Rackliff'** is a compact grower with white flowers. ZONES 7–9.

Erica mammosa
Red signal heath

This South African species has bright green foliage and, in spring, massed terminal clusters of red to deep pink tubular flowers, each 1 in (25 mm) long. It grows to about 3 ft (1 m) high and 18 in (45 cm) wide.

Erica erigena 'Ewan Jones'

Erica erigena 'Hibernica Alba'

Erica erigena 'Superba'

Erica mammosa

'**Coccinea**' is a particularly heavy-flowering cultivar, while '**Jubilee**' has pink flowers. ZONES 9–10.

Erica vagans
Cornish heath

This vigorous, spreading, European species, 30 in (75 cm) high and wide, has deep green foliage and rounded, bell-shaped, pink, mauve or white flowers, borne in clusters in summer and autumn. The cultivar, '**St. Keverne**' bears a profusion of clear pink flowers. ZONES 5–9.

Erica mammosa 'Jubilee'

Erica erigena 'W. T. Rackliff'

Erica vagans

EXOCHORDA

Pearl bush

There are 4 species of deciduous shrubs in this genus from central Asia and northern China. They have weak, pithy branches and thin-textured, paddle-shaped leaves. In spring, the branch ends are clustered with 5-petaled, white flowers of delicate, informal beauty. The fruits are capsules with wing-like segments, splitting apart when ripe to release flattened seeds. **CULTIVATION** Species of *Exochorda* are quite frost hardy, but they prefer climates with sharply defined seasons and dry summers for the best display of flowers. A sheltered position in full sun and well-drained soil are desirable. Prune older stems back to their bases after flowering for vigorous new growth and abundant flowers. Propagate from seed in autumn or from cuttings.

Exochorda × macrantha 'The Bride'

Exochorda × macrantha

This hybrid was raised in France around 1900 by crossing *Exochorda racemosa* with the central Asian *E. korolkowii*. Sometimes reaching 10 ft (3 m) tall, in mid- to late spring it produces elongated clusters of pure white flowers, each about 1½ in (35 mm) across, from every branch tip. **'The Bride'** is one of the loveliest varieties of pearl bush. It makes a weeping shrub about 6 ft (1.8 m) tall and wide and it bears masses of large white flowers on arching stems in spring. ZONES 6–9.

Exochorda × macrantha

FG

FORSYTHIA

Since their introduction to Western gardens from China and Japan in the nineteenth century, the seven species of *Forsythia* are popular shrubs valued for their brilliant yellow or gold blossoms in mid-spring. They make excellent cut flowers. Deciduous or sometimes semi-evergreen and of medium stature, they have soft-wooded stems branching from near the ground. The rather narrow, bluntly toothed leaves appear after the 4-petaled flowers, which are paired or clustered at the twig nodes. **CULTIVATION** Fully frost hardy, they are not fussy about soil type, but fertilizer and compost encourage growth. They prefer a sunny position, and climate is crucial: they seldom flower in warm climates, requiring winter temperatures well below freezing point. Prune only to remove older branches. Propagation is normally from cuttings in early summer.

Forsythia × intermedia
Border forsythia

An arching or spreading deciduous shrub with dark green, lance-shaped leaves, this species grows 8–10 ft (2.4–3 m) tall and slightly wider. A hybrid between *Forsythia suspensa* and *F. viridissima,* it was originally recorded in Germany in 1885. Some

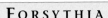
Useful Tip

The seed of some shrubs from dry areas needs exposure to fire to initiate germination. Try keeping them in a fish smoker for an hour or so, or mix with cooling ashes.

Forsythia × intermedia

Forsythia × *intermedia* 'Lynwood'

fine cultivars include '**Lynwood**' and '**Spectabilis**'. In 1939, at the Arnold Arboretum in Massachusetts,

Forsythia × *intermedia* 'Spectabilis'

Forsythia × *intermedia* 'Arnold Giant'

Karl Sax created the first artificial tetraploid, '**Arnold Giant**', and subsequently bred '**Beatrix Farrand**' and '**Karl Sax**', all carrying large, brilliant gold flowers. ZONES 5–9.

FREMONTODENDRON

syn. *Fremontia*
Flannel bush

This unusual genus consists of two species of evergreen or semi-evergreen shrubs or small trees from the far southwestern USA and Mexico. The young stems have a felty coating of hairs, as do the lobed leaves on their pale undersides. The large, bowl-shaped flowers consist of 5 large, petal-like, golden sepals. They are named after Major-General John Charles Fremont (1813–90), a distinguished American explorer and amateur botanist.
CULTIVATION Frost hardy, these plants are not difficult to grow in a sheltered, sunny position with neutral to alkaline, well-drained soil, but they tend to be short lived. Plant out in spring. They do not perform well in climates with hot, wet summers. Propagate from seed in spring or cuttings in summer.

Fremontodendron californicum

This is the best known and hardiest species, originating from California's

Sierra Nevada foothills and coastal ranges. Although it can reach 30 ft (9 m), it is usually a sparse, crooked shrub about 20 ft (6 m) tall, with dark brown bark. It produces a succession of 2 in (5 cm) wide golden flowers from mid- to late spring. *Fremontodendron californicum* subsp. *decumbens* has a dwarf habit and orange-yellow flowers. ZONES 8–10.

Fremontodendron californicum

FUCHSIA

This genus consists of about 100 species—mostly from Central and South America—and thousands of hybrids and cultivars, developed for their pendulous flowers, which come in a fascinating variety of forms (usually with a long or short perianth tube, spreading sepals and 4 broad petals) and a wonderful range of colors. They are evergreen or deciduous trees, shrubs or perennials treated almost as herbaceous plants. Most of the larger-flowered American species inhabit areas of very high rainfall, sometimes growing as epiphytes or on boulders in moss forests; they are pollinated by hummingbirds. Habit varies from upright shrubs to spreading bushes. Trailing lax varieties are ideal for hanging baskets. Strong upright types may be trained as compact bushes, standards or espaliers.

CULTIVATION Moderately frost hardy to frost tender, these plants require moist but well-drained, fertile soil in sun or partial shade and shelter from hot winds and afternoon sun. In most instances, pinching back at an early age and then pruning after flowering will improve shape and flower yield. Propagate from seed or cuttings, and check for white fly, spider mite, rust and gray mold.

Fuchsia magellanica
Ladies' eardrops, hardy fuchsia

From Chile and Argentina, this vigorous, erect shrub grows up to

Fuchsia magellanica

Fuchsia magellanica 'Thompsonii'

Fuchsia Hybrid

10 ft (3 m) tall. It has lance-shaped
to ovate leaves, commonly held in
whorls of three. The pendulous,
red, tubular flowers with red sepals
and purple petals are produced over
a long period in summer; black
fruit follow. Prune it back to maintain its shape. '**Alba**' can grow to a
considerable size and bears white
flowers. '**Thompsonii**' has scarlet
tubes and sepals and pale purplish
petals; although the flowers are

smaller than type, they are more
profuse. '**Versicolor**' (syn. 'Tricolor')
has gray-green leaves that are flushed
red when immature and irregularly
white-splotched margins when
mature; the flowers are small and
deep red. ZONES 7–10.

Fuchsia Hybrids
syn. *Fuchsia* × *hybrida*

This name covers the thousands
of modern, large-flowered hybrid

Fuchsia magellanica 'Versicolor'

Fuchsia 'Baby Blue Eyes'

Fuchsia 'Blue Satin'

Fuchsia 'Tango Queen'

cultivars derived mainly from *Fuchsia magellanica, F. fulgens* and *F. triphylla*. 'Baby Blue Eyes', 'Blue Satin', 'Jack of Hearts' and 'Tango Queen' are typical hybrids. All may be grown in pots, hanging baskets or planted in the garden. Those of upright habit may be trained as standards. ZONES 8–11.

Fuchsia 'Jack of Hearts'

GREVILLEA

Some 250 species of evergreen shrubs and trees make up this genus. Variable in habit, foliage and flowers, most grevilleas are native to Australia. The small flowers are mostly densely crowded into heads or spikes, their most conspicuous feature being the long styles, which are at first bent over like a hairpin and then straighten out. Many are adaptable and easy to grow, with a long flowering period, and are popular with nectar-seeking birds. The leaves are commonly deeply divided and may be very decorative in their own right. In the last several decades, hundreds of hybrid grevillea cultivars have been bred and

Grevillea lanigera 'Mt. Tamboritha'

many are extremely floriferous. Some of the most beautiful species are low growing or prostrate; these may be planted in a rock garden, as ground cover, or in pots. CULTIVATION Moderately frost hardy to frost tender, grevilleas do best in full sun, in well-drained, slightly dry, neutral to acid soil. Strong roots develop early and it is important not to disturb these when planting out. Pruning of shrubby species and cultivars is recommended immediately after flowering to promote healthy

new growth and a compact habit. They are generally pest free although scale insects and leaf spot may pose a problem. Propagate from seed in spring, from cuttings in late summer, or by grafting for some of the species most prone to root-rot.

Grevillea lanigera
Woolly grevillea

This species has narrow, grayish, furred leaves and red and cream flower clusters from late winter to spring. It varies in size—some forms are prostrate and others grow to about 3 ft (1 m) tall and wide. This is one of the most frost-hardy species, but it does resent summer humidity. 'Mt. Tamboritha' is a small, prostrate form with soft gray-green foliage and reddish pink and cream flowers. ZONES 7–9.

Grevillea victoriae
Royal grevillea

This variable species is an upright, spreading shrub to 6 ft (1.8 m) high and 10 ft (3 m) across. It has ovate, gray-green leaves to 6 in (15 cm) long with silvery undersides. Pendent clusters of rusty red, spider-type flowerheads appear in spring and again in late summer and autumn. Occurring at elevations of up to 6,000 ft (1,800 m), it is one of the most frost-hardy grevilleas. ZONES 7–9.

Grevillea victoriae

HK

HEBE

Veronica

With over 100 species of evergreen shrubs, the hebes include many first-rate garden plants. They have neat, attractive leaves and often showy flower-spikes, which arise in the axils of the leaves, as in '**Autumn Beauty**' and '**Pamela Joy**'. There are 2 main groups of hebes. The first is the broad-leafed hebes, fast-growing shrubs with pleasing foliage and abundant spikes of small flowers, ranging from white through pink to violet and blue, over a long summer to autumn season. The second group, the whipcord hebes, have small leaves that give them the appearance of dwarf conifers, and white or pale mauve flowers.

CULTIVATION Most hebes are best suited to temperate to warm climates. In warm climates, they grow equally well in sun or shade; in cooler climates, sun is preferred. They like moist but well-drained soil; the broad-leafed types benefit from a post-flowering trim. Many mountain whipcord hebes are not easy to grow at low altitudes. Protect from strong winds. Propagate from cuttings in summer.

Hebe 'Autumn Beauty'

Hebe 'Pamela Joy'

Hebe speciosa

Hebe 'Wiri Mist'

Hebe speciosa
Showy hebe

Hebe speciosa is an evergreen compact shrub, which grows from 2 to 5 ft (0.6 to 1.5 m) high, spreading to 4 ft (1.2 m) wide in a broad, bun shape. It has oval, glossy foliage and bears a profusion of reddish purple flowers in terminal clusters from early summer to late autumn. This species is more prone to wilt than other hebes. Many attractive cultivars exist, including **'Variegata'**, with creamy white leaf margins; all tolerate some frost. ZONES 9–10.

Hebe 'Wiri Joy'

Hebe, Wiri Hybrids

This showy, large-flowered, rounded shrub, is densely clothed with glossy, oblong leaves. Purple-pink flowers appear in summer. **'Wiri Mist'** grows to 18 in (45 cm) and spreads to 3 ft (1 m). It has thick, yellow-margined green leaves and bears an abundance of white flowers toward the end of spring. ZONES 8–11.

HIBISCUS

While the genus name conjures up the innumerable cultivars of *Hibiscus rosa-sinensis,* the genus of around 220 species is quite diverse, including hot-climate evergreen shrubs and small trees and also a few deciduous, temperate-zone shrubs and some annuals and perennials. The leaves are mostly toothed or lobed and the flowers, borne singly or in terminal spikes, are of singular shape: a funnel of

5 overlapping petals and a central column of fused stamens.

CULTIVATION Easy to grow, the shrubby species thrive in sun and slightly acid, well-drained soil. Water regularly and feed during the flowering period. Trim after flowering to maintain shape. Propagate from seed or cuttings or by division, depending on the species. Check for aphids, white fly and mealybugs. The *H. rosa-sinensis* cultivars are good greenhouse subjects in frosty climates, and compact cultivars are gaining popularity as house plants.

Hibiscus rosa-sinensis

Chinese hibiscus, red hibiscus, shoeflower

This is a glossy leafed, evergreen shrub, sometimes as much as 15 ft (4.5 m) high and wide, with blood red flowers borne almost all year. It is less often seen than its numerous garden cultivars, some pure bred and others, like the enormous blooming Hawaiian hybrids, carrying the genes of other species. These plants grow 3–10 ft (1–3 m) high, and the

Hibiscus rosa-sinensis 'Surfrider'

flowers can be 5-petaled singles, semi-double or fully double, the colors ranging from white through pinks to red; the Hawaiian hybrids offer yellow, coral and orange, often with 2 or 3 shades in each flower. The flowers range upwards in size from about 5 in (12 cm); some of the Hawaiian hybrids are as large as dinner plates. Each flower lasts only a day, opening in the morning and withering by evening, but they appear in long succession as long as the weather is warm. All the *Hibiscus rosa-sinensis* cultivars like a frost-

Useful Tip

If you don't need the seeds of your shrubs, remove spent flowerheads immediately. Setting seed is a major drain on a plant's resources.

Hibiscus rosa-sinensis 'Fiesta'

Hibiscus rosa-sinensis 'Covakanic'

Hibiscus syriacus 'Diana'

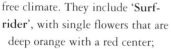

free climate. They include '**Surf-rider**', with single flowers that are deep orange with a red center; '**Fiesta**', with dark apricot flowers with red and white centers; '**Covakanic**', with flowers in beautiful varying tones of orange and apricot; as well as '**Apple Blossom**', '**Cooperi**', '**Madonna**' and '**Sabrina**'. ZONES 10–12.

Hibiscus syriacus
Blue hibiscus, rose of Sharon

This upright, deciduous shrub (ever-green in warmer climates) from temperate Asia is the most frost hardy of the genus. It flowers freely in summer in varying shades of white, pink, soft red, mauve and violet blue. The single, semi-double and double flowers are bell-shaped and are borne in the axils of the leaves. The plant has small, hairless leaves and grows to 12 ft (3.5 m) tall with a spread of 3–6 ft (1–1.8 m). Prune to shape in the first 2 years of growth, trimming lightly there-after to maintain a compact form. Popular cultivars of *Hibiscus syriacus* include '**Ardens**', with large, mauve flowers with crimson centers; '**Blue**

Hibiscus syriacus 'Blue Bird'

Hibiscus syriacus 'Woodbridge'

Bird', with single, violet blue flowers with red centers; 'Diana', with broad, pure white flowers; and 'Woodbridge', with two-toned pink blooms at least 4 in (10 cm) across. ZONES 5–10.

HYDRANGEA

These deciduous or evergreen shrubs, climbers and sometimes small trees occur over a wide area of temperate Asia and North and South America. Most species have large, oval leaves with serrated edges; some develop good autumn color. The flower clusters contain tiny, fertile flowers and showy, sterile ones with 4 petal-like sepals. Although most species produce panicles of flowers with few sterile flowers, many cultivated forms have heads composed almost entirely of sterile flowers. Flower color may vary with the acidity or alkalinity of the soil: blue in acid soil, pink or red in alkaline; white cultivars do not change. In some, but not all cultivars, the old flowers gradually fade to shades of green and pink, this color being independent of soil type.
CULTIVATION Except in cool, moist climates, they need shade or part-shade or both leaves and flowers will scorch; and though soil should be constantly moist

Hydrangea aspera

and rich in humus, it should be well drained. Pruning is best done immediately after bloom. Propagation is usually from cuttings or seed. Check regularly for powdery mildew, leaf spot, honey fungus and pests such as aphids, scale insects and spider mites.

Hydrangea aspera

This species occurs naturally over much of southern and eastern Asia, showing much variation in the wild. In cultivation it grows to around 10 ft (3 m) high and wide. Its serrated-edged leaves vary from

Useful Tip

Always check potential plant heights and light requirements before planting. It is very easy to unintentionally shade out a smaller plant with a taller one.

Hydrangea macrophylla

Hydrangea macrophylla 'Sir Joseph Banks'

Hydrangea macrophylla 'Altona'

narrow to oval, and are 3–10 in
(8–25 cm) long. The large flowerheads appear in summer and are

H. m. 'Générale Vicomtesse de Vibraye'

lacecap style with pale, sterile
flowers and tiny, purplish blue,
fertile flowers; color varies little
with soil type. The **Villosa Group**
bears broad heads of blue or purple
flowers in the center of the shrubs
and larger white flowers toward the
periphery. They are very frost hardy.
ZONES 7–10.

Hydrangea macrophylla
Bigleaf hydrangea, garden
hydrangea

This species in its wild form is un-
common in cultivation. However,

Hydrangea macrophylla 'Blue Sky'

Hydrangea macrophylla 'Blue Wave'

Hydrangea macrophylla 'Libelle'

the name also covers a large race of garden varieties derived from it, though in fact many of these may have originated as hybrids between *Hydrangea macrophylla* and *H. aspera.* The group known as "hortensias" have flowerheads of the mophead type, with densely massed, sterile florets. Examples include '**Altona**', with flowers that vary from deep pink to purplish blue; '**Générale Vicomtesse de Vibraye**' bears large flowerheads in pink or pale blue; and pink-flowered '**Sir Joseph Banks**'. A smaller group is the

"lacecaps;" examples include '**Blue Sky**', '**Blue Wave**' and '**Geoffrey Chadbund**', which has rich, bright red flowers. '**Libelle**' has extra large, pure white, infertile flowers that give the head a crowded, full look; '**Lilacina**' has pink flowers that may be tinged purple; '**Shower**' produces elegant blooms of clear, hot pink; '**Sunset**' is a big, vigorous shrub which often grows to over 5 ft (1.5 m) across and produces many heads of rich pinkish scarlet blooms; and '**Taube**', similar to '**Sunset**', but smaller, and with softer pink

H. macrophylla 'Geoffrey Chadbund'

Hydrangea macrophylla 'Shower'

Hydrangea macrophylla 'Sunset'

Hydrangea paniculata 'Grandiflora'

blooms. **'Veitchii'** bears flowers opening white and ageing to soft pink. ZONES 6–10.

Hydrangea paniculata
Panicle hydrangea

This deciduous shrub from China and Japan grows to 15 ft (4.5 m) or more, with a broad, dome-shaped crown the same in width. It has large, oval, dark green leaves and in midsummer bears small, cream, fertile flowers and larger flat, creamy white, sterile flowers that turn rose

purple as they age. Prune hard in late winter or spring for larger blooms. **'Grandiflora'** is the form most commonly grown. **'Tardiva'** flowers in autumn. ZONES 5–9.

Hydrangea quercifolia
Oak-leaf hydrangea

Native to the USA, this deciduous shrub grows to a height of 6–8 ft (1.8–2.4 m), spreading by stolons to 12 ft (3.5 m) or more. Deeply lobed, dark green leaves turn an orange-scarlet in autumn. The

Hydrangea macrophylla 'Taube'

Hydrangea paniculata 'Tardiva'

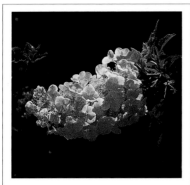

Hydrangea quercifolia

flowers, borne from midsummer to midautumn, are a mixture of small, fertile and sterile flowers. The white, sterile flowers fade to pink and violet. It performs best in dappled shade. ZONES 5–9.

HYPERICUM

St. John's wort

This is a large and varied genus of 400 species of annuals, perennials, shrubs and a few small trees, some evergreen but mostly deciduous. Hypericums have showy flowers in shades of yellow with a central mass of prominent golden stamens. They are found throughout the world in a broad range of habitats. Species range in size from tiny perennials for rockeries to specimens over 10 ft (3 m) tall. CULTIVATION Mostly cool-climate plants, they prefer full sun but will tolerate some shade. They do best in fertile, well-drained soil, with plentiful water in late spring and summer. Remove seed capsules after flowering and prune in winter to maintain a rounded shape. Cultivars are propagated from cuttings in summer, and species from seed in autumn or from cuttings in summer. Some species are susceptible to rust.

Hypericum calycinum
Aaron's beard, creeping
St. John's wort

One of the best of all ground covers for temperate climates, this species from Turkey is a low-growing, evergreen shrub, about 15 in (38 cm) tall, that spreads rapidly by creeping, runner-like stems to cover quite a large area. The midsummer flowers are about the size of a rose and have long stamens. Any sort of soil suits and, though the plant will grow happily in the dry shade beneath deciduous trees, it flowers more profusely if given sunshine. ZONES 6–10.

Hypericum calycinum

Hypericum 'Hidcote'

Hypericum 'Hidcote'

This dense bushy shrub reaches 4 ft (1.2 m) in height and has a spread of 5 ft (1.5 m). It bears large, cup-shaped, $2\frac{1}{2}$ in (6 cm) golden yellow flowers from midsummer to early autumn, and has lance-shaped, dark green leaves. ZONES 7–10.

KOLKWITZIA

Beauty bush

This genus consists of a single species of deciduous shrub from China, much admired in temperate and cool-climate gardens for its lavish spring display. Since its foliage is undistinguished during summer, however, it should be placed where other plants can attract the eye.

CULTIVATION Fully frost hardy, *Kolkwitzia* grows in any well-drained soil and does well in sun or light shade. It can become very untidy if old wood is not removed from time to time; winter pruning will simply cut away the flowering wood. Propagation is from cuttings in summer.

Kolkwitzia amabilis

This bushy shrub develops into a mass of upright, cane-like stems to 12 ft (3.5 m) high. The leaves are in opposite pairs, oval, $1\frac{1}{2}$ in (35 mm) long and deep green. The pale pink, trumpet-shaped flowers, which open in spring, form profuse clusters at the ends of the side branches. They are followed by small fruit covered with bristles. 'Pink Cloud' has clear pink flowers and is slightly larger than the type. ZONES 4–9.

Kolkwitzia amabilis

LM

LAVANDULA

Lavender

These fragrant, evergreen, aromatic shrubs, of which there are around 25 species, are valued for their attractive lacy, fragrant, usually grayish foliage. They occur naturally from the Mediterranean region through the Middle East as far as India. Most species grow 24–36 in (60–90 cm) high, with a similar spread. The small, mauve-purple or bluish purple flowers emerge from between bracts in erect, short spikes held on stalks above the foliage; flowering occurs mostly in spring. There are oil glands at the bases of the flowers that produce the pungent oil of lavender, obtained commercially by distillation from *Lavandula angustifolia* and *L. stoechas*.
CULTIVATION These plants prefer full sun and fertile, well-drained soil; they will thrive in both acid and alkaline soils. The woodier species, such as *L. dentata*, are excellent as low hedges, and a light trim after blooming keeps them neat. Hardiness varies with the species, although most are moderately frost hardy if the growth is well ripened by warm autumn weather. Propagate from seed or cuttings in summer.

Lavandula angustifolia
syn. *Lavandula officinalis*,
L. spica, L. vera
Lavender

This dense, bushy subshrub grows to about 3 ft (1 m) tall—though usually lower—with narrow, furry gray leaves. It is grown mainly for the long-stemmed heads of purple, scented flowers that appear in summer and through the warm

Lavandula angustifolia 'Munstead'

Lavandula angustifolia 'Alba'

months; these are easily dried for lavender sachets, potpourri and the like. *Lavandula angustifolia* makes an attractive low hedge and can be trimmed after flowering. There are a number of selected cultivars, of which '**Munstead**' and the dwarf '**Hidcote**' are outstanding. '**Alba**' grows to 24 in (60 cm) with a 3 ft (1 m) spread; it has pale gray-green foliage and white flowers in whorls. '**Jean Davis**' grows to 15–18 in (38–45 cm) and has blue-green foliage and tall, pinkish white flowers. ZONES 6–10.

Lavandula dentata

Densely packed, soft spikes of mauve-blue flowers remain on this shrub from autumn through to late spring in warm climates. A native of the western Mediterranean and Atlantic islands, its gray-green aromatic leaves are fern-like with blunt teeth or lobes. It grows to a height and spread of 3–4 ft (1–1.2 m). A marginally frost-hardy species, resistant to dry conditions and adaptable to most soils, it is often used as an edging plant to soften the harsh lines of paving. ZONES 8–10.

Lavandula stoechas
Spanish lavender, French lavender

This marginally frost-hardy species is the most striking in flower of all lavenders, at least in some of its varied forms. A small, neat shrub, 20–30 in (50–75 cm) high, it has pine-scented, narrow silvery green leaves with inward-curling edges. In late spring and summer it is covered with spikes of deep purple

Lavandula dentata

Lavandula stoechas

Lavandula stoechas subsp. *lusitanica*

flowers. Several bracts at the apex of each spike are elongated into pinkish purple "rabbit ears" of varying size. 'Merle' is a compact bush with long-eared, magenta-purple flowerheads. 'Marshwood' is a very heavy flowering, long-blooming cultivar. *Lavandula stoechas* subsp. *lusitanica* has very narrow leaves and dark purple flowers with paler "rabbit ear" bracts. *L. stoechas* subsp. *pedunculata* (syn. *L. pedunculata*) grows 18–24 in (45–60 cm) tall,

Lavandula stoechas subsp. *pedunculata*

has greenish foliage, and its flower spikes are plump and pale green after the flowers drop. *L. stoechas* subsp. *luisieri* is an upright bush with green, rather than silver-gray, foliage and large, purple flower spikes. ZONES 7–10.

MAGNOLIA

This large, varied genus of 100 or more species of deciduous and evergreen trees and shrubs from East Asia and the Americas was named after French botanist Pierre Magnol. Magnolia leaves are commonly oval and smooth edged. The flowers are generally large, fragrant and solitary, come in pink, white, yellow or purple, and vary in shape from almost flat and saucer-like to a narrow goblet shape. The fruits are cone-like or roughly cylindrical.
CULTIVATION Magnolias require deep, fertile, well-drained soil. Some species require alkaline soil; others prefer a mildly acid, humus-rich soil. The roots are fragile so the plants do not transplant easily. They thrive in sun or part-shade but need protection from strong or salty winds. The flower buds are particularly frost sensitive. Propagation is from cuttings in summer or seed in autumn, or by grafting in winter.

Magnolia liliiflora

Magnolia stellata

Magnolia liliiflora

syn. *Magnolia quinquepeta*

Lily magnolia

A deciduous, bushy shrub, this Chinese species reaches 10 ft (3 m) tall and 15 ft (4.5 m) wide. The mid- to dark green leaves, downy on the undersides, taper to a point. Fragrant, narrow, purplish pink flowers, whitish inside, are borne among the leaves from midspring until midsummer. 'Nigra' has large, dark wine purple flowers that are pale purple inside. ZONES 6–10.

Magnolia stellata

Star magnolia

This many-branched, compact, deciduous shrub from Japan grows 10–15 ft (3–4.5 m) tall and wide, with aromatic bark when young, and narrow, dark green leaves. Starlike, white, fragrant flowers open from silky buds in late winter and early spring, before the leaves. It flowers when young, and has several cultivars in shades of pink, including 'Rosea'. The prolific flowerer, 'Waterlily', has more petals and larger, white flowers. ZONES 5–9.

Magnolia liliiflora 'Nigra'

Magnolia stellata 'Rosea'

P

PAEONIA

Peony

There are 33 species in this genus of beautiful perennials and shrubs. Peonies are all deciduous and have long-lived, woody rootstocks with swollen roots, and large compound leaves with usually toothed or lobed leaflets. Each new stem in spring terminates in one to several large, rose-like flowers. Their centers are a mass of short stamens that almost conceal the 2 to 5 large ovaries, which develop into short pods containing large seeds. The flowers are mostly in shades of pink or red, but there are also white and yellow-flowered species. The great majority of peonies are herbaceous, dying back to the ground in autumn, but there is a small group of Chinese species, known as the "tree peonies," that have woody stems. These grow no more than about 8 ft (2.4 m) in height, so strictly they are shrubs. Cultivars of this tree peony group produce the largest and most magnificent of all peony flowers, some approaching a diameter of 12 in (30 cm); they are mostly double and often beautifully frilled or ruffled.

CULTIVATION Although most peonies will only succeed in climates with a cold winter, allowing dormancy and initiation of flower buds, new foliage and flower buds can be damaged by late frosts. They appreciate a sheltered position in full or slightly filtered sunlight, but with soil kept cool and moist. Mulch and feed with well-rotted manure when leaf growth starts, but avoid disturbing roots. Pruning of the tree peonies should be minimal, consisting of trimming out weaker

Useful Tip

Always keep records, even very brief ones; it's amazing how easy it is to forget what you have planted or when you last sprayed. Save any labels or seed packets with your notes.

Paeonia suffruticosa

Paeonia suffruticosa hybrid

side shoots. Propagate from seed in autumn, or by division in the case of named cultivars. Tree peony cultivars are best propagated from basal suckers, but few are produced, hence plants on their own roots are very expensive. A faster and cheaper method is to graft them onto herbaceous rootstocks, but the resulting plants are often disappointingly short lived.

Paeonia suffruticosa
Tree peony, moutan

Native to China, this handsome deciduous shrub has been so avidly transplanted into gardens it is quite possibly extinct in the wild. It reaches a height and width of 3–6 ft (1–1.8 m) and produces very large, single or double, cup-shaped flowers in spring. Depending on the variety, these are white, pink, red or yellow, and are set among attractive, large, mid-green leaves. *Paeonia suffruticosa* subsp. *rockii* has semi-double, white flowers with a maroon blotch at the base of each petal. ZONES 4–9.

PELARGONIUM

The genus *Pelargonium* consists of perhaps 280 species, the vast majority endemic to southern Africa. Although pelargoniums are mostly soft-wooded shrubs and subshrubs, some are herbaceous perennials or even annuals; there is also a large but little known group of species that have succulent stems, leaves

Paeonia suffruticosa subsp. *rockii*

or roots and are grown by collectors of succulents. The leaves of pelargoniums are often as broad as they are long and are variously toothed, scalloped, lobed or dissected, depending on species; they are usually aromatic, containing a wide range of essential oils, and may secrete resin droplets which give the leaves a sticky feel.

CULTIVATION Frost tender, these plants are often treated like annuals for summer bedding in colder climates. In warmer climates with long hours of daylight, they flower almost all the time, although they do not do well in extreme heat and humidity. Plant in pots or beds. The site should be sunny with light, well-drained, neutral soil. If grown in pots, fertilize and deadhead regularly. Propagate from softwood cuttings any time from spring to autumn.

Pelargonium, Regal Hybrids

Martha Washington geraniums, regal geraniums, regal pelargoniums

The spectacular, large blooms of these hybrids make them suitable for exhibiting in flower shows. Sprawling shrubs, growing about 24 in (60 cm) high, they have strong woody stems and stiff, pleated, sharply toothed leaves. In late spring and summer, they bear clusters of large flowers, wide open and often blotched or bicolored. Frost tender,

Pelargonium, Regal Hybrid, 'Kimono'

in cool areas they need a greenhouse. Cut back hard after blooming to keep the bushes compact. **'Grand Slam'** is heavy flowering and compact, with flowers a deep pinkish red suffused salmon pink with darker markings and a small white center. **'Kimono'** is bright pink with darker markings and a white center. **'Lord Bute'** is black-red with lighter edges. **'Lyewood Bonanza'** is white with apricot-pink markings on the upper petals.

Pelargonium, Regal Hybrid, 'Lord Bute'

P., Regal Hybrid, 'Lyewood Bonanza'

Pelargonium, Regal Hybrid, 'Parisienne'

P., Regal Hybrid, 'Monkwood Bonanza'

'**Monkwood Bonanza**' is pale pastel pink with darker markings. '**Morwenna**' (syn. 'Morweena') has deep maroon flowers shading to near black. '**Parisienne**' has mauve flowers with purple and blackish red markings on the upper petals. '**Rembrandt**' has some of the largest and most richly colored flowers: deep purple with frilled, lavender edges. '**Rosmaroy**' is bright pink with reddish markings. '**Spot-on-Bonanza**' is white or

Pelargonium, Regal Hybrid, 'Morwenna'

Pelargonium, Regal Hybrid, 'Rembrandt'

Pelargonium, Regal Hybrid, 'Rosmaroy'

Pelargonium, Regal Hybrid, 'White Glory'

P., Regal Hybrid, 'Spot-on-Bonanza'

Pelargonium, Regal Hybrid, 'Vicky Clare'

pale pink with flecks or sectors of apricot pink. **'Vicky Clare'** has multi-colored blooms, deep purple-red on the upper petals, pink veining on the lower and the whole edged in white. **'White Glory'** is pure white. **'Starlight Magic'** has velvety, purple-pink petals above and a paler shade beneath. ZONES 9–11.

PHILADELPHUS

Mock orange, syringa

This genus of 60 species of deciduous shrubs comes from the temperate regions of the Northern Hemisphere. The cultivated species are all quite similar. They grow to a height and spread of 10 ft (3 m) and have light green, roughly elliptical leaves about 3 in (8 cm) long. They flower in late spring

Philadelphus 'Miniature Snowflake'

Philadelphus 'Natchez'

and early summer, bearing white or cream 4-petaled flowers in loose clusters. The flower scent strongly resembles that of orange blossom, hence the common name. '**Miniature Snowflake**' is a dwarf cultivar of the popular '**Snowflake**', and '**Natchez**' is another cultivar often grown.

CULTIVATION Moderately to very frost hardy, they are easily grown, preferring moist, well-drained soil and a position in sun or light shade. *Philadelphus* may be pruned after flowering and can be used for informal hedging. Propagate from seed or from cuttings taken in summer.

Philadelphus coronarius

From southern Europe and Asia Minor, this species grows to 6 ft (1.8 m) tall, and has very fragrant 2 in (5 cm) wide, white flowers. Its

Philadelphus coronarius

Philadelphus coronarius

Philadelphus 'Virginal'

oval, bright green leaves are slightly hairy on the undersides. **'Aureus'** has bright yellow new growth and smaller flowers; **'Variegatus'** bears white flowers and has white-edged leaves. ZONES 2–9.

Philadelphus 'Virginal'

Very frost hardy, this vigorous, upright shrub grows to a height and spread of a little under 10 ft (3 m). From late spring to early summer, it bears large, fragrant, semi-double, white flowers set among dark green, oval leaves. ZONES 3–9.

regions. Most species have 5-part leaves, hence the common name "cinquefoil," and range from only 1 in (25 mm) or so tall to about 18 in (45 cm). They bear clusters of 1 in (25 mm), rounded, bright flowers in profusion through spring and summer. Some of the *Potentilla* species are used medicinally: the root bark of one species is believed to stop nose bleeds and even internal bleeding. **CULTIVATION** Plant all species in well-drained, fertile soil. Lime does not upset them. Although the species all thrive in full sun

POTENTILLA

Cinquefoil

This genus of approximately 500 perennials, annuals, biennials and deciduous shrubs is indigenous mainly to the Northern Hemisphere, from temperate to Arctic

Useful Tip

For a rough and ready test of soil pH, sprinkle a teaspoon of baking soda over a small, wetted soil sample. If it bubbles or fizzes, the soil is acidic; if not it is alkaline.

Potentilla fruticosa

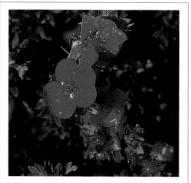

Potentilla fruticosa 'Goldstar'

in temperate climates, the colors of pink, red and orange cultivars will be brighter if protected from very strong sun. Perennials are generally frost hardy. Propagate by division in spring, or from seed or by division in autumn. Shrubs can be propagated from seed in autumn or from cuttings taken in summer.

Potentilla fruticosa
Bush cinquefoil

This dense, deciduous shrub, found in many parts of the temperate Northern Hemisphere, grows to over 3 ft (1 m) tall, with a spread of 4 ft (1.2 m) or more. From early summer to autumn, garden varieties bear 1 in (25 mm) wide flowers in shades from white to yellow and orange, the orange ones often fading to salmon pink in the sunshine. The flat, mid-green leaves comprise 5 or 7 narrow, elliptical leaflets, arranged palmately. There are many popular cultivars available. '**Tangerine**' has golden orange flowers; '**Goldstar**' is an upright shrub with large,

Potentilla fruticosa 'Tangerine'

Potentilla fruticosa 'Maanleys'

Potentilla fruticosa 'Elizabeth'

deep yellow flowers; and **'Maanleys'** reaches 4 ft (1.2 m) tall with blue-green foliage and pale yellow flowers. **'Abbotswood'** is a very attractive, spreading, 24 in (60 cm) tall shrub with white flowers; **'Beesii'** grows to 24 in (60 cm) tall with very silvery leaves and bright yellow flowers; **'Daydawn'** is a 3 ft (1 m) tall shrub with salmon-pink flowers; **'Elizabeth'** is a dense, bushy, 3 ft

Potentilla fruticosa 'Beesii'

Potentilla fruticosa 'Primrose Beauty'

Potentilla fruticosa 'Goldfinger'

(1 m) shrub with bright yellow flowers; '**Goldfinger**' is a low grower with narrow, bright green leaflets and very bright yellow flowers; and '**Primrose Beauty**', up to 3 ft (1 m) tall and 5 ft (1.5 m) wide, bears primrose-yellow flowers, reminiscent of a small wild rose. ZONES 2–9.

PRUNUS

This large genus of 430 species, mostly from the Northern Hemisphere, includes the edible stone fruits—cherries, plums, apricots, peaches, nectarines and almonds —but there are also ornamental species and cultivars with beautiful flowers. The genus includes several shrubby species, but the majority are trees. Most of the familiar species are deciduous and bloom in spring (or late winter in mild climates) with scented, 5-petaled, pink or white flowers.

The leaves are simple and often serrated and all species produce a fleshy fruit containing a single hard stone.

CULTIVATION Plant in moist, well-drained soil in full sun. Plants should be placed where spring blossoms are protected from strong winds. Propagate by grafting or from seed; named cultivars must be grafted or budded onto seedling stocks. Pests and diseases vary with locality.

Prunus glandulosa
Dwarf flowering almond, almond-cherry

This deciduous species belongs to a group of dwarf *Prunus* species that are part of the cherry subgenus *(Cerasus)* but show some of the attributes of almonds and peaches. It makes a showy, late spring-flowering shrub of up to 5 ft (1.5 m), with thin, wiry branches, small leaves, and profuse white to pale pink flowers, borne along the stems. The dark red fruit is about half the size of a cherry and although edible, is rather sour. It is common practice to cut the bushes back almost to ground level as soon as flowering finishes, producing a thicket of strong vertical shoots that bloom freely the next spring. '**Sinensis**' (syn. 'Rosa Plena') bears double pink flowers and '**Alba Plena**' has double white flowers. ZONES 6–10.

R

RHODODENDRON

syn. *Azalea*

Rhododendron is a diverse genus of deciduous, semi-evergreen and evergreen trees and shrubs, totaling some 800 species with thousands of cultivars. There are three divisions: azaleas, vireyas and "true" rhododendrons, ranging from miniature shrubs to small trees. Flowers come in a range of colors. The bell- to funnel-shaped flowers have 5 or more petals and are usually held in clusters at the branch tips. In some cultivars either the calyx or stamens develop into petal-like structures, known as "hose in hose."

CULTIVATION Most require part-shade and prefer light, well-drained but moist soil with a slightly acid pH, enriched with organic matter with a cool root run. They are intolerant of lime. Protect from the afternoon sun and strong winds. They are prone to infestation by two-spotted mite (red spider mite), thrips and powdery mildew in humid areas.

Propagate from cuttings, or by layering or grafting.

Rhododendron calendulaceum
Flame azalea

This deciduous azalea, found from West Virginia to Georgia, USA, develops into a spreading bush around 12 ft (3.5 m) tall and wide. Its orange to red (rarely yellow), funnel-shaped flowers open in late spring and are carried in trusses of 5 to 7 blooms. The flower color varies with the season, location and climate. Many orange to flame azaleas derive their color from this species. ZONES 5–9.

Rhododendron calendulaceum

Rhododendron catawbiense

Rhododendron catawbiense
Catawba rhododendron,
mountain rosebay

This shrub from eastern USA is one of the most influential species in the development of frost-hardy hybrids. It grows to around 10 ft (3 m) tall and develops into a dense thicket of shiny, deep green foliage. Its cup-shaped flowers, which open from late spring, may be pink, rosy pink, lilac-purple or white and are carried in trusses of up to twenty blooms. 'Album' is a heat-resistant form with white flowers that open from pink buds. ZONE 4–9.

Rhododendron degronianum

This rhododendron grows into a neat small shrub, 4–6 ft (1.2–1.8 m) high, with a domed crown. It produces dark green leaves up to 6 in (15 cm) long with light brown, fuzzy undersides. Its bell-shaped flowers are a delicate, soft pink and appear in late spring. *Rhododendron degronianum* subsp. *Yakushimanum* is a dense, mounding shrub, 3–8 ft (1–2.4 m) tall, with 3–4 in (8–10 cm) long, deep green, leathery leaves with rolled edges and heavy fawn indumentum. The flowers appear quite early and are white or

Rhododendron degronianum

pale pink, opening from deep pink buds and carried in rounded trusses of up to 10 blooms. 'Exbury Form' makes a perfect dome of deep green, heavily indumented foliage with light pink flowers. 'Koichiro Wada' is similar to 'Exbury Form', but has white flowers opening from deep pink buds. ZONES 7–9.

Rhododendron fortunei

This Chinese species has been extremely influential in the development of garden hybrids. It is a shrub or small tree, 4–30 ft (1.2–9 m) tall, with matt, mid-green oval leaves up to 8 in (20 cm) long. Its fragrant, 4 in (10 cm) wide flowers open pink and fade to white. They open from midspring and are carried in large, rounded trusses.

Rhododendron fortunei subsp. *fortunei*

Rhododendron fortunei subsp. **discolor** has flowers with a yellow-green throat blotch; **R. f.** subsp. **fortunei** has scented, pale pink to lavender flowers. ZONES 6–9.

Rhododendron kiusianum

The foliage of this azalea develops yellow, red and purple tones as it

Rhododendron kiusianum

Rhododendron luteum hybrid

ages and most of the oval, hairy leaves are dropped by the end of winter, despite its classification as an evergreen. A very dense, twiggy bush that forms a rounded hummock to around 3 ft (1 m) high and 5 ft (1.5 m) wide, from early spring it is hidden beneath masses of tiny pinkish purple flowers. White and light pink-flowered

Rhododendron molle subsp. *japonicum*

forms are also available. This is one of the parents of the Kurume azalea hybrids. ZONES 6–10.

Rhododendron luteum

This deciduous azalea grows to 12 ft (3.5 m) and has 2–4 in (5–10 cm) long, bristly, lance-shaped leaves. Its flowers are bright yellow and sweetly scented. They are long and funnel-shaped with a narrow tube and form trusses of up to 12 blooms. ZONES 5–9.

Rhododendron molle

This deciduous azalea from China grows 4–6 ft (1.2–1.8 m) tall and, from midspring, bears large, densely packed trusses of 2½ in (6 cm) long, funnel-shaped, yellow or orange flowers. The flowers are sometimes fragrant. ***Rhododendron molle*** subsp.

japonicum (syn. *R. japonicum*), from Japan, is a 3–10 ft (1–3 m) tall shrub with bright red, orange-red, pink or yellow flowers and brightly colored autumn foliage. This subspecies is the principal parent of the deciduous Mollis azaleas. ZONES 7–9.

Rhododendron nakaharai

This evergreen Taiwanese azalea is a near-prostrate shrub, usually under 12 in (30 cm) tall. The pointed, elliptical leaves are hairy and a little under 1 in (25 mm) long. Small, orange-red, funnel-shaped flowers, 1 in (25 mm) long, open in early summer. This is a good rockery, bonsai or ground-cover plant. 'Mt. Steven Star' is a densely foliaged, prostrate form with large orange-red flowers. ZONES 5–10.

Rhododendron occidentale

From western USA, this species is a 6–15 ft (1.8–4.5 m) tall deciduous azalea with slightly hairy, 4 in (10 cm) long, elliptical leaves. The fragrant 3 in (8 cm) wide, funnel-shaped flowers are carried in trusses of up to 12 blooms, and are usually white or pale pink with a yellow, occasionally maroon, flare, although it may be red, yellow or orange-pink. The autumn foliage is coppery red. The cultivar **'Leonard Frisbie'** has large, frilled, fragrant flowers that are white suffused pink with a yellow flare. ZONES 6–10.

Rhododendron nakaharai

Rhododendron ponticum

From Europe and the Middle East to Russia, this 6–20 ft (1.8–6 m) shrub has glossy, deep green, oblong to lance-shaped leaves up to 8 in (20 cm) long. The 10- to 15-flowered trusses open in late spring and are 2 in (5 cm) long, funnel-shaped, purple, lavender, pink or rarely maroon or white flushed pink, often with yellow, ochre or brown flecks.

Rhododendron ponticum

Rhododendron ponticum

It is used in hybridizing. 'Variegatum' has dark green leaves with cream edges and occasional stripes or flecks. ZONES 6–10.

Rhododendron schlippenbachii
Royal azalea

This deciduous azalea is a 6–15 ft (1.8–4.5 m) tall shrub with 4–6 in (10–15 cm) long leaves in whorls of five. Its 3- to 6-bloom trusses of 3 in (8 cm) wide flowers, which are usually lightly scented and open in

Rhododendron, Kurume A., 'Addy Wery'

midspring, vary from white flushed pink to rose pink, often with brown flecks. The foliage colors well in autumn. It prefers light shade. ZONES 4–9.

Rhododendron williamsianum

This densely foliaged shrub grows 2–5 ft (0.6–1.5 m) tall and has rounded to heart-shaped, matt mid-green leaves up to 2 in (5 cm) long. The new growth is a contrasting bronze color. The flowers, which appear in midspring, are bell-shaped, 2 in (5 cm) long, mid-pink to rose, sometimes with darker flecks and are carried in loose clusters of 2 to 3 blooms. ZONES 7–9.

Rhododendron, Kurume Azaleas

Kurume azaleas are dense, compact growers with small leaves and a mass of petite flowers early in the

Rhododendron, Kurume A., 'Fairy Queen'

Rhododendron, Kurume A., 'Hinodegiri'

season. Many Kurume azaleas have hose-in-hose flowers in which the sepals become petal-like and create the effect of a second corolla. Most are best grown in full sun or very light shade; they respond well to trimming to shape after flowering. **'Addy Wery'**, 5 ft (1.5m) tall, has deep orange-red, single flowers and bronze winter foliage. **'Christmas Cheer'** (syn. 'Ima Shojo'), 3 ft (1 m) tall if trimmed, otherwise 6 ft (1.8 m), is a compact bush cloaked in tiny, vivid cerise, hose-in-hose flowers. **'Fairy Queen'** (syn. 'Aioi'),

3 ft (1 m) tall, is a compact shrub with pale apricot-pink, hose-in-hose flowers often with a red blotch. **'Hatsu Giri'**, 4 ft (1.2 m), is a twiggy, upright bush with vivid purplish flowers that are occasionally spotted pink. **'Hino Crimson'**, 5 ft (1.5 m) tall, has bright pinkish red, single flowers that often hide the foliage, and is among the last to bloom. **'Hinodegiri'**, 5 ft (1.5 m) tall, is a dense, heavily foliaged shrub that produces masses of tiny cerise single flowers. **'Hinomayo'** (syn. 'Hinomoyo'), 6 ft (1.8 m) tall,

Rhododendron, Kurume Azalea, 'Hatsu Giri'

Rhododendron, Kurume Azalea, 'Kirin'

Rhododendron, Kurume Azalea, 'Osaraku'

is a strong-growing bush with vivid purple-pink single flowers. '**Iroha Yama**' (syn. 'Dainty'), 4 ft (1.2 m) tall, is a compact bush with single white flowers that have deep apricot-pink edges. '**Kirin**' (syn. 'Coral Bells') is certainly one of the best of the Kurumes and probably the most popular azalea of all. It is a dense, heavily foliaged bush with rounded, bright green leaves that become bronze in winter. From very early spring it becomes a solid mass of soft pastel pink, hose-in-hose flowers and grows to 3 ft (1 m) if

trimmed, otherwise 6 ft (1.8 m) or more. '**Osaraku**' (syn. 'Penelope'), 5 ft (1.5 m) tall, has single flowers with very delicate shadings of white suffused light purple. '**Red Robin**' (syn 'Waka Kayede'), 3 ft (1 m) tall, is a spreading bush that glows with single, bright orange-red flowers from midspring. '**Sui Yohi**' (syn. 'Sprite'), 6 ft (1.8 m) tall, has delicately shaded and textured, single, white flushed pale pink flowers with pink petal tips. This is one of the more frost-tender Kurumes. '**Venus**', 6 ft (1.8 m) tall, is a

Rhododendron, Kurume Azalea, 'Red Robin'

Rhododendron, Kurume Azalea, 'Venus'

Rhododendron, Hardy Hybrid, 'Britannia'

R., Hardy Hybrid, 'Furnival's Daughter'

Kurume × Indica cross, but is most often listed as a Kurume. It produces an abundance of small, reddish blooms. The somewhat frost tender 'Ward's Ruby', which grows to 5 ft (1.5 m) tall, is usually regarded as the deepest-red-flowered evergreen azalea; its flowers are small and single. ZONES 7–10.

Rhododendron, Hardy Hybrids

These are the most widely grown of all the rhododendrons. Hardy Hybrids, although mostly large, domed shrubs with sizeable, dull green leaves, do in fact vary considerably in size, from low spreading bushes to small trees. They flower spectacularly in spring, bearing many almost spherical clusters of wide open flowers in whites, pinks, reds and purples, rarely cream or yellow. There are many named cultivars, varying from frost hardy to fully hardy. Some examples include 'Blue Peter', 'Britannia', 'Furnival's Daughter' and 'Mrs. G. W. Leak'. The usual conditions of cultivation for rhododendrons apply. ZONES 4–9.

Rhododendron, Hardy Hybrid, 'Blue Peter'

R., Hardy Hybrid, 'Mrs. G. W. Leak'

ROSA

Rose

About 140 species make up the genus *Rosa*, all of them native to the Northern Hemisphere. Roses are divided into 3 groups: Old Garden Roses, Modern Garden Roses and Wild Roses. There are many thousands of hybrids and garden cultivars, which are arranged in a variety of flower forms, and in every shade of pink, red, white, yellow, orange, mauve, purple and coral; that is, every color but true blue. Cultivars can also be blends and variegations of two or more colors. Fragrance among cultivars ranges from almost none to an intense, almost exotic fragrance. Size of plants also varies from a few inches (centimeters) to giant, scrambling roses. When choosing a rose it is best to check neighbors' gardens and local nurseries to see which roses grow best in your particular area.

Rosa californica

CULTIVATION Roses prefer cool to cool-temperate conditions and sunny positions, which reduces the incidence of fungal diseases such as mildew, black spot and rust. They require a fairly rich, deep soil and slow, deep watering during long, dry spells. Roses should be mulched, fertilized twice yearly (spring and summer) and any suckers removed from rootstocks or standard stems. They are prone to aphids, mites and thrips. Propagate from stratified seed (Wild Roses), cuttings from well-ripened branches, layering, or by budding.

Rosa, Wild Roses

Of the 140 species of Wild Roses, only a few are common in gardens, including **Rosa chinensis**, a repeat-flowering, near-evergreen shrub or scrambler, growing 4–8 ft (1.2–2.5 m) high and wide. It bears 5-petaled flowers, usually in small

Rosa foetida

Rosa californica 'Plena'

Rosa rugosa

groups, that open pink and rapidly age to red, followed by orange hips; it is suited to Zones 7–11. *R. foetida* is a deciduous species which develops into a dense, twiggy shrub up to 5 ft (1.5 m) high and wide with numerous prickles. Its flowers are 5-petaled and bright yellow. *R. californica*, a vigorous shrub growing to 10 ft (3 m) tall, has soft, dull green leaves with 5 to 7 broadly elongated leaflets and small corymbs of blooms produced over a longish period from early summer; the color is mid-pink with little or no scent. The plumply oval hips, which are red when ripe, follow in autumn. *R. californica* is a useful shrub for wild gardens; it appears to be hardy in all but the coldest areas. A semi-double form, '**Plena**', is a decorative garden shrub which freely produces lilac-pink flowers and orange-red fruit. *R. rugosa* has a dense, bushy habit and grows to about 8 ft (2.5 m) high and wide.

It blooms in repeated flushes over a long season. The 5-petaled, deep pink flowers are followed by showy, large, pinkish orange-red hips. This hardy, disease-resistant species has given rise to a group of hybrids known collectively as Rugosas. *R. rugosa alba* is a larger, white-flowered form. ZONES 3–10.

Rosa, Old Garden Roses

Old Garden Roses are those roses of a style or parentage pre-dating the introduction of the first of the Large-flowered roses (Hybrid Teas),

Rosa rugosa alba

Rosa, OGR, Alba, 'Alba Maxima'

Rosa, OGR, Damask, 'Ispahan'

around 1860. Within this classification, there are individual groups of roses, each group having a distinctive feature or origin. One of the most popular groups is Gallica Roses, derived primarily from *Rosa gallica*, including **'Anaïs Ségales'**, a small bush with once-flowering, deep pink, double flowers. Albas are "white roses" such as **'Alba Maxima'**, up to 8 ft (2.4 m) tall, with showy, once-flowering, double flowers. The Damasks include the once-flowering Summer Damasks, and the Autumn Damasks, which

flower in summer and have a limited second flowering in autumn. Examples include **'Omar Khayyám'** and **'Ispahan'**, both fragrant mid-pink doubles. Centifolias, the "one hundred-petaled roses" raised by Dutch hybridists in the seventeenth century, include **'Petite de Hollande'**, a small bush with masses of strongly scented, pink blooms, and **'Fantin-Latour'**, with glorious powdery pink blooms. Moss Roses have a most attractive mossy excrescence on the stems and the sepals. Mosses include **'Crested**

Rosa, OGR, Damask, 'Omar Khayyám'

Rosa, OGR, Centifolia, 'Fantin-Latour'

Rosa, OGR, Moss, 'Crested Moss'

R., OGR, Bourbon, 'Souvenir de St. Anne's'

Moss' (syn. 'Chapeau de Napoléon'), with fragrant, mid-pink, double flowers. China Roses are a significant group of repeat-flowering roses and include '**Mutabilis**', with butterfly-like, yellow blooms that age pink through to crimson. The Tea Roses, a group valued for their graceful and fragrant blooms, include '**Lady Hillingdon**', with loose double, apricot-yellow flowers. Bourbon Roses were the first repeat-flowering roses to be created from the Chinas. The Bourbons include '**Souvenir de St. Anne's**', '**Queen** of Bourbons' (syn. 'Bourbon Queen'), and '**Boule de Neige**', with white double flowers opening from pink-striped buds. Portland Roses are repeat-flowering, the result of a cross of Gallica, Damask, Centifolia and China roses; an example is '**Comte de Chambord**', with sweetly scented, pink, double flowers. Hybrid Perpetuals, a repeat-flowering group which resulted from intense hybridization, includes '**Champion of the World**', a deep pink double that is always one of the first to bloom.

Rosa, OGR, Tea, 'Lady Hillingdon'

Rosa, OGR, Bourbon, 'Boule de Neige'

Rosa, MGR, Large-flowered, 'Peace'

Rosa, MGR, Large-flowered, 'Just Joey'

Rosa, **Modern Garden Roses**

Most roses grown today are Modern Garden Roses, from which there are many, many to choose. They are classified as **Bush Roses** (Large-, Cluster-flowered or Polyantha) which make compact, upright bushes about 3 ft (1 m) tall and often more in mild climates. **'Peace'** is a Large-

Rosa, MGR, Cluster-fl., 'Auckland Metro'

flowered rose with perfectly formed, soft yellow flowers edged rose pink. **'Auckland Metro'**, **'Just Joey'**, **'Double Delight'**, **'Mme. Caroline Testout'**, **'Loving Memory'** and **'Tequila Sunrise'** are other popular Large-flowered roses. **'Iceberg'** is covered in heads of pure white blooms over a long season; the full blooms of **'Bordure Rose'** (syn. 'Strawberry Ice') have beautiful, creamy petals rimmed with pink; and **'Burma Star'**, **'Playboy'**, and **'Ripples'** are other popular Cluster-flowered roses.

Rosa, MGR, Large-flowered, 'Loving Memory'

Rosa, MGR, L-f, 'Mme. Caroline Testout'

Rosa, MGR, Shrub, 'Stretch Johnson'

Shrub Roses are taller, less upright growers, mostly repeat flowering, and include the stunning '**Jacqueline du Pré**', '**Stretch Johnson**' (syn.'Rock 'n' Roll'), and '**Fritz Nobis**', growing to 6 ft (1.8 m) tall, with clusters of pale pink to white, semi-double flowers. '**Buff Beauty**' has flowers of soft yellow, ageing to cream, and '**Autumn Delight**' bears soft creamy yellow blooms with beautiful golden stamens; both are Hybrid Musks. '**Sarah van Fleet**' is a tall, prickly

Rosa, MGR, Cluster-flowered, 'Iceberg'

Rosa, MGR, Large-flowered, 'Tequila Sunrise'

Rosa, MGR, 'Fritz Nobis'

Rosa, MGR, Hybrid Musk, 'Buff Beauty'

Rosa, MGR, English, 'Constance Spry'

bush with scented, double, deep pink flowers, and '**Roseraie de l'Haÿ**' has crimson-purple blooms

Rosa, MGR, English, 'Charles Austin'

with an exotic fragrance; both are Hybrid Rugosas. English Roses include '**Charles Austin**', with large, fragrant blooms in a dusky buff to yellow shade and '**Constance Spry**', an exceptionally popular rose with soft luminous pink, cup-shaped, double flowers. **Miniature Roses** make lovely shrubs, including '**Anita Charles**', with deep pink, double flowers and an amber reverse to the petals; and '**Si**', the smallest of all roses, which produces exquisite pink rosebuds. ZONES 5–10.

Rosa, MGR, Miniature, 'Anita Charles'

Rosa, MGR, Miniature, 'Si'

ST

SPARTIUM

Spanish broom

This genus includes just a single species: a deciduous, almost leafless shrub that is indigenous to the Mediterranean region. The crushed flowers are used to make a yellow dye.

CULTIVATION This adaptable plant thrives in well-drained soil enriched with a little organic matter. Full sun is best. It is a shrub suited to warm to coolish climates. Pruning after flowering will maintain compact, well-shaped bushes. Propagate either from seed or cuttings.

Spartium junceum

This shrub bears masses of large, golden yellow, fragrant pea-flowers carried in loose, 18 in (45 cm) long spikes at the shoot tips. It flowers profusely through spring into early summer. The leaves are narrow, bluish green and less than 1 in (25 mm) long; they are shed from the new growth soon after they appear. Spanish broom makes a bushy shrub 6–10 ft (1.8–3 m) tall; on older specimens, the stems arch downwards. The fruits are flat, silvery pods maturing to brown. ZONES 6–11.

Spartium junceum

SPIRAEA

This genus consists of 80 species of deciduous or semi-evergreen shrubs, popular for their spring and summer flower display and their autumn foliage. They form clumps of wiry stems that shoot up from the base and are densely covered with narrow, toothed leaves. Spiraeas belong to the rose family and, examined under a magnifying glass, the flowers do resemble tiny roses but they are so small that the individual flower is lost among the mass of blooms carried on each flower cluster.

CULTIVATION Spiraeas are adaptable plants that thrive under most garden conditions in temperate climates, though they prefer a warm summer. They thrive in moist, well-drained soil and a position sheltered from the hottest sun, especially in warm-summer areas where the foliage may burn. Most spiraeas should be pruned

Spiraea japonica

after flowering. Propagation is from cuttings taken in summer.

Spiraea japonica
Japanese spiraea

This low, mounding, deciduous shrub bears rose pink to red flowers from late spring to midsummer. It grows to a height and spread of about 6 ft (1.8 m). The cream and

Spiraea japonica 'Anthony Waterer'

Spiraea japonica 'Goldflame'

pink variegated new leaves turn green as they mature. It has the best foliage of any in the genus. There are many varieties and cultivars, including 'Little Princess', to 3 ft (1 m) tall; 'Anthony Waterer', the most commonly cultivated selection; 'Goldflame', popular for its bronze new growth that turns golden as it matures; 'Nyewoods', with small leaves and dark pink flowers; 'Shirobana', with both dark pink and white flowers on the one plant; and 'Nana' (syn. 'Alpina'), more compact at 18 in (45 cm) tall. ZONES 3–10.

Spiraea japonica 'Nana'

SYRINGA

Lilac

Lilacs are prized for their upright to arching panicles of small, highly fragrant flowers, which are massed in loose heads. They appear from midspring and range from white and pale yellow to all shades of pink, mauve and purple. Most of the common garden varieties of *Syringa vulgaris* were raised in France in the late 1800s to early 1900s, though new forms appear from time to time. Not all cultivars are fragrant. The genus contains about 20 species, all deciduous shrubs and trees from Europe and northeastern Asia. Most reach about 8 ft (2.4 m) high and 6 ft (1.8 m) wide, with opposite leaves that sometimes color well in autumn.

CULTIVATION Lilacs prefer moist, humus-rich, well-drained soil in sun or light shade. They do best where winters are cold, because they require at least a few frosts in order to flower well. Any pruning is best done immediately after flowering. Species may be raised from seed or cuttings. Named cultivars are ordinarily grafted but can sometimes be struck from hardwood or semi-ripe cuttings. Established plants produce suckers that can be used for propagation.

Useful Tip

Many flowering shrubs make excellent hedges; try Chaenomeles, Philadelphus, *certain roses and, for a vivid spring show, plant some* Rhododendron kiusianum.

Syringa × persica 'Alba'

Syringa × persica
Persian lilac

This is thought to be a hybrid of *Syringa laciniata* and *S. afghanica* or else a stable juvenile form of *S. laciniata*. Probably indigenous to Afghanistan, Persian lilac is a deciduous, bushy, compact shrub. In spring, it bears profuse heads of small, delightfully fragrant flowers, set amid narrow, pointed, dark green leaves. It grows to a height and spread of just under 6 ft (1.8 m); it grows better in warmer winter climates than do most other lilacs. 'Alba' has dainty, sweetly scented, white flowers. ZONES 5–9.

Syringa vulgaris
Common lilac

Most garden cultivars derive from this species. It is native to southeastern Europe and grows to about 20 ft (6 m) high with pointed, oval or heart-shaped leaves up to 4 in (10 cm) long. The strongly fragrant,

S. vulgaris 'Andenken an Ludwig Späth'

S. vulgaris 'Andenken an Ludwig Späth'

Syringa vulgaris 'Mme. Lemoine'

Syringa vulgaris 'Louis van Houtte'

white or pale mauve flowers are produced in dense pyramidal heads. '**Andenken an Ludwig Späth**' (syn. 'Souvenir de Louis Spaeth') has single, deep purple, large flowerheads in mid-season; '**Katherine Havemeyer**' has fully double, large-flowered heads of lavender-purple buds opening to a soft mauve-pink; '**Mme. Lemoine**' is a double white form with medium-sized, tight flowerheads on a free-flowering and compact shrub; and '**Primrose**' has early, single, lemon flowers on a compact shrub. Other popular cultivars include '**Mme. F. Morel**' and 'Louis van Houtte'. ZONES 5–9.

TAMARIX

Tamarisk

The fifty or so species of tough shrubs and small trees in this genus occur naturally in southern Europe, North Africa and temperate Asia, growing in dry riverbeds, often in saline soils. Most *Tamarix* species are deciduous, but a few are evergreen. They develop a short trunk and a graceful, dense canopy of drooping branchlets. The leaves, which are minute and scale-like, have salt-secreting

Syringa vulgaris 'Mme. F. Morel'

Useful Tip

For maximum water efficiency, group shrubs with similar water requirements and ensure that any surrounding annuals and perennials have similar needs.

glands. The small, white or pink flowers occur in abundant, slender spikes; the fruits are capsules. **CULTIVATION** Grown for ornament and as windbreaks, tamarisks adapt to a wide range of soils and climates and can cope with salt spray and very dry conditions.

Very to moderately frost hardy, they do best in deep, sandy soil with good drainage and can be pruned after flowering. Propagate from ripe seed or from hardwood cuttings in winter, and semi-ripe cuttings in late spring or autumn. They are prone to attack by stem borers in poorly drained soil.

Tamarix tetrandra

This species grows to 10 ft (3 m), with arching purplish brown shoots and needle-like leaves. In spring, it bears lateral racemes of 4-petaled, pink flowers on the previous year's growth. ZONES 6–10.

Tamarix tetrandra

VW

VIBURNUM

This important genus is made up of some 150 species of evergreen, semi-evergreen and deciduous cool-climate shrubs or small trees, primarily of Asian origin, with fewer species from North America, Europe and northern Africa. Many of the cultivated species and forms are noted for their fragrant, showy flowers and may produce colorful berries or bright autumn foliage. In several species, flowers are arranged in a similar way to those of the lacecap hydrangeas, with small fertile flowers and large sterile ones on the same plant; these have all given rise to cultivars with all-sterile flowerheads known as "snowball viburnums." The evergreen species are often used for hedging.

CULTIVATION Fully to moderately frost hardy, most species are remarkably trouble-free plants, growing in any well-drained soil in sun or light shade. They can be trimmed heavily after flowering, although this will prevent fruit forming. Viburnums are propagated either from cuttings in summer or seed in autumn.

Viburnum × burkwoodii
Burkwood viburnum

A hybrid between *Viburnum carlesii* and *V. utile,* this 8–10 ft (2.4–3 m) high, semi-evergreen shrub has glossy, deep green, pointed oval leaves to about 3 in (8 cm) long. They are pale sage green on the undersides and those that drop in autumn develop bright yellow and red tones. From early to late spring, ball-shaped clusters of small, starry, fragrant flowers open; they are pink in the bud, opening white.

Viburnum × burkwoodii

Viburnum × burkwoodii 'Park Farm'

Viburnum carlesii 'Aurora'

'**Anne Russell**', the result of a backcross with *V. carlesii*, has clusters of fragrant flowers, and '**Park Farm**' has a more spreading habit and larger flowers. '**Mohawk**' has dark, glossy leaves that turn to orange in autumn and fragrant, red-blotched, white flowers that open from red buds. ZONES 5–10.

Viburnum carlesii

Korean viburnum, Korean spice viburnum

Indigenous to Korea and Tsushima Island, this densely

foliaged deciduous shrub grows to about 5 ft (1.5 m) tall with a similar spread. It has pointed oval leaves, 2–3 in (5–8 cm) long, with finely serrated edges. The starry flowers open from mid- to late spring; they are pale pink ageing to white, around $\frac{1}{2}$ in (12 mm) across, and sweetly scented. The flowers are carried in rounded clusters up to 3 in (8 cm) in diameter. The fruits ripen to black. Several cultivars are available, including '**Aurora**', with deep pink buds; '**Cayuga**', which has fragrant white flowers and a

Viburnum carlesii

Viburnum opulus

Viburnum opulus 'Aureum'

Viburnum opulus 'Roseum'

heavy crop of black berries; **'Charis'**, bearing white flowers; and **'Diana'**, with deep pink buds. ZONES 9–10.

Viburnum opulus

Guelder rose, European cranberry bush

This lovely deciduous shrub from Europe and North Africa produces splendid clusters of snowy white, lacy flowers in summer. It has attractive fruit and autumn color, and can be grown in wet or boggy situations. A large shrub, growing to 12 ft (3.5 m) tall, it has gray bark and a spreading habit with long, pale green shoots. Its leaves turn deep crimson in autumn. Generous bunches of shiny, translucent, orange-red fruit remain on the bush until well into winter. Cultivars include **'Aureum'**, with bronze-colored shoots turning yellow then green, and yellowish leaves which may burn in the sun; **'Compactum'**, a dense, compact shrub bearing large quantities of flowers and fruit; **'Roseum'** (syn. *Viburnum opulus* 'Sterile'), the snowball bush, has snowball-like heads

Viburnum opulus 'Compactum'

Viburnum opulus 'Pink Sensation'

Weigela 'Bristol Ruby'

of pale green to white, sterile flowers so large they weigh the branches down; '**Pink Sensation**', similar to 'Roseum', except the flowers have a pinkish hue; and '**Xanthocarpum**', with clear yellow fruit which are quite translucent when ripe. ZONES 2–10.

WEIGELA

This genus includes about twelve species of arching, deciduous shrubs native to Japan, Korea and northeastern China. Most grow 6–10 ft (1.8–3 m) high and wide, and have pointed, elliptical, deep green leaves about 4 in (10 cm) long. The foliage often develops orange, red and purple tones in autumn. In spring, masses of attractive, pink, crimson or white, sometimes yellowish, bell- or trumpet-shaped flowers appear, each 1½ in (35 mm) long.

CULTIVATION Fully frost hardy, most species prefer full sun or light shade in moist, fertile, well-drained soil. Prune out the older branches soon after flowering to maintain vigor. Propagation is from summer cuttings.

Weigela 'Bristol Ruby'

This erect hybrid, bred from *Weigela florida* and *W. coraeensis*, is grown for the profusion of crimson flowers that adorn the shrub from late spring to early summer. It grows to 6 ft (1.8 m) tall, with slender, arching branches and dark green, oval leaves. ZONES 4–10.

Weigela florida

Weigela florida 'Eva Rathke'

Weigela florida 'Aureovariegata'

Weigela floribunda
syn. *Diervilla floribunda*

This deciduous shrub from Japan reaches about 10 ft (3 m) in height and has slender, pointed leaves that are hairy on both sides. The young shoots are also hairy, as are the outsides of the flowers. The deep crimson flowers are tubular in form, with styles projecting out from the opened petals; they are crowded on short lateral branchlets. ZONES 6–10.

Weigela florida
This arching, deciduous shrub grows to 3 m (10 ft) or so tall. It is cultivated for its lavish spring display of rose pink, trumpet-shaped flowers. 'Aureovariegata' has bright green, cream-edged leaves and clear pink, trumpet-shaped flowers to 1½ in (35 mm) wide. 'Eva Rathke'

grows 1.5 m (5 ft) tall and wide, with a dense, erect habit and bears crimson flowers. The flowers of 'Foliis Purpureis' are deep pink, paler inside the tube and appear from late spring to early summer and sometimes again in autumn. ZONES 4–10.

Weigela florida 'Foliis Purpureis'

HARDINESS ZONE MAPS

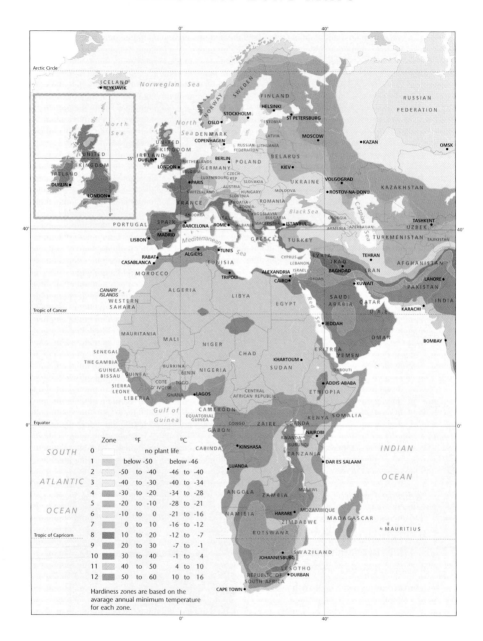

Zone	°F	°C
0	no plant life	
1	below -50	below -46
2	-50 to -40	-46 to -40
3	-40 to -30	-40 to -34
4	-30 to -20	-34 to -28
5	-20 to -10	-28 to -21
6	-10 to 0	-21 to -16
7	0 to 10	-16 to -12
8	10 to 20	-12 to -7
9	20 to 30	-7 to -1
10	30 to 40	-1 to 4
11	40 to 50	4 to 10
12	50 to 60	10 to 16

Hardiness zones are based on the
avarage annual minimum temperature
for each zone.

Note: The scale of this map differs from that of the following two maps.

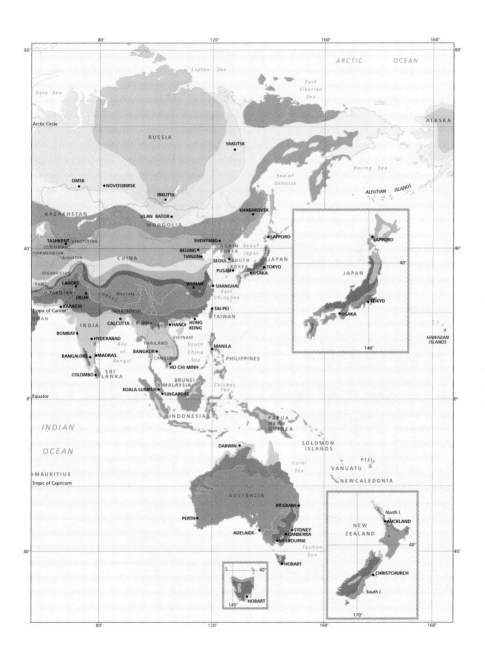

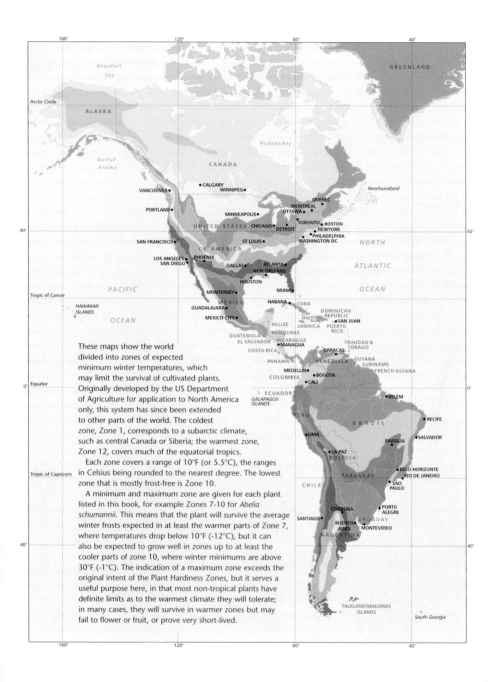

These maps show the world divided into zones of expected minimum winter temperatures, which may limit the survival of cultivated plants. Originally developed by the US Department of Agriculture for application to North America only, this system has since been extended to other parts of the world. The coldest zone, Zone 1, corresponds to a subarctic climate, such as central Canada or Siberia; the warmest zone, Zone 12, covers much of the equatorial tropics.

Each zone covers a range of 10°F (or 5.5°C), the ranges in Celsius being rounded to the nearest degree. The lowest zone that is mostly frost-free is Zone 10.

A minimum and maximum zone are given for each plant listed in this book, for example Zones 7-10 for *Abelia schumannii*. This means that the plant will survive the average winter frosts expected in at least the warmer parts of Zone 7, where temperatures drop below 10°F (-12°C), but it can also be expected to grow well in zones up to at least the cooler parts of zone 10, where winter minimums are above 30°F (-1°C). The indication of a maximum zone exceeds the original intent of the Plant Hardiness Zones, but it serves a useful purpose here, in that most non-tropical plants have definite limits as to the warmest climate they will tolerate; in many cases, they will survive in warmer zones but may fail to flower or fruit, or prove very short-lived.

INDEX